THE IDEA
OF CRITICISM

ι

THE PENNSYLVANIA STATE
UNIVERSITY STUDIES NO. 20

THE IDEA OF CRITICISM

by Albert Tsugawa

THE PENNSYLVANIA STATE UNIVERSITY
University Park, Pennsylvania

PN 81
.T76

91181

to the memory of
Paul Henle

ACKNOWLEDGMENTS

The help that I have received while this study was in progress is so widespread that it would be difficult to name all of my friends, colleagues and teachers from whom I have learned and whose teachings have flowed into this study. The following persons, however, have been especially generous with their time in discussing problems with me, and in reading earlier versions of some of the chapters and in commenting on them: Charles Caton, Henry Harris, Peter Stettenheim, William W. Hartney, and Stanford Tsugawa. I am grateful to John M. Anderson and Henry W. Johnstone for their encouragement and help while the work was in preparation. I have received grants from the Central Fund for Research of The Pennsylvania State University which have aided me in the completion of this manuscript. A version of Chapter 5 (part of which is here included in Chapter 6) was originally published in the *Philosophical Review* for January, 1961. Permission to quote from copyrighted material has been generously granted by the following: Alfred A. Knopf, Inc. for *Harmonium* by Wallace Stevens, Constable Publishers for *Medieval Latin Lyrics* by Helen Waddell, and the Oxford University Press, Inc. for *The Poems of Gerard Manley Hopkins*.

CONTENTS

INTRODUCTION

The title of this work is apt. In it I examine the idea of criticism as applied to works of art. What criticism is and how it is possible comprise the theme of the book. I begin with actual criticism. Thus, the chief focus is on the arguments and reasons formulated by critics and on what they understand criticism to be and think that it can achieve. What they say, how they argue, how they use their expertise, the sort of ground they provide to make good their assertions, how they can mediate their differences: these are some of the things I wish to discuss. I propose in the beginning to keep the discussion away from living works of art and turn the attention on criticism and the methods of critics. From such an investigation, one can unearth a set of presuppositions about the nature of works of art: what critics presume art to be, notions that must be posited to support critical procedure and make criticism itself possible.

The study begins with a consideration of styles of criticism in general. What do the critics propose to accomplish in their larger design? Does the idea of criticism adhered to by a critic make a difference in his tactics and in his general strategy? Will this idea affect the data of the art work on which he will concentrate?

The main purpose, however, of the study is to determine the nature of critical discourse: to decide upon the extent to which it includes as essential the formulation of considerations and reasons; the extent to which it includes analysis of works of art; whether and how description and interpretation are involved in critical discourse. A discussion of these questions helps us to deal with the problems of the objectivity of criticism and the irreducibly subjective elements in it. In critical discourse, too, we find the problem of the nature of aesthetic judgments which includes the standards and criteria on which they are based and the question of their universality.

The focus of attention, as indicated, will be on the methods and results of critics. In this respect, the task is partly descriptive and taxonomic. The goal is to achieve conceptual clarity and to reveal the logical and factual relationship of concepts of criticism, their affinities as well as their antipathies. Furthermore the task is partially Platonic and legislative as well — to sketch the ideal map of the critical terrain. Therefore it is necessary to draw distinctions where critics in their normal discourse may have failed to draw them and to suggest what seems to be the essential nature of aesthetic arguments.

There is a relationship, though not an obvious one, between criticism and aesthetics. As the examination of the language of criticism proceeds, a number of aesthetic concepts and philosophic notions recur. Thus, after completion of the discussion of the logic of criticism, it is possible to clarify some of these concepts and notions, primarily by showing their interrelationships. In the final chapter, some of these concepts are briefly discussed in order to suggest the definition of art that seems to underlie the theory of criticism.

I REASON AND CRITICISM

1 | THE IDEA OF CRITICISM

Talk constitutes criticism, but criticism should not attempt to usurp the place of a work of art. Nothing can do that. Criticism that does not leave the work of art whole and intact for full contemplation and appreciation is bad. When we criticise, we speak out. It is a discursive activity, bringing to our awareness our commerce with works of art. However, what we say needs to be scrutinized against the reality of works of art. Criticism that makes this impossible is faulty discourse; yet according to some anti-critics, analysis destroys a work of art. But what sort of reasoning can it be that destroys what we talk about in the very process of reasoning?

The aims of criticism must be modest though it may have consequences that reach beyond these modest aims. Primarily, the purpose of the critic is to share what he has experienced in his study of works of art. One may wonder what need there is to talk about an experience one has had. Yet this need is natural. On the crudest level, it shows up in the conversations of persons leaving a concert.

A Wasn't that a wonderful concert?

B Indeed it was. Such a nice group of selections!

C The second half of the concert went off better than the first half.

B   I agree, but I thought the Schubert Quartet might have been played more romantically — it should have dripped with emotion.

C   Well, maybe the performers were a bit reserved, but they aren't Germans.

Conversations like this may merely serve to prolong the emotions of the concert. Then they are only the pious ceremonial expression of togetherness. But words uttered with care and sensitivity can open up the experience of one person to another. Comparing what I saw and felt with what another person saw and felt (perhaps someone no more but no less careful and experienced than I) can have intrinsic as well as practical interest. It is, for one thing, a way of estimating the adequacy of my own responses. If I discover to my surprise that my experience was different from another person's, I might want to know why. The cause of the differences is worth discovering, and subsequent discussion might reveal it.

We enjoy discussing films, novels, etc., that have held us spellbound, and the talk can be endless, especially when they are a bit complicated or meaty. Not only do I enjoy describing my own responses and expounding my own interpretations, but I also like to exchange remarks and get other viewpoints. We may even go back to see a film or reread a novel. Much of the fascination is in the exercise of our own imaginations; but provided we do not suffer from monomania, the contents of the minds of others can be interesting too. Oftentimes, in such discussions, there is a working toward intersubjectivity, though there may not be great care in the use of expression, nor much accuracy in the descriptions. We learn, in this process, to pay attention to other people's responses, and we also learn that disagreements in responses and judgments disturb us. How often have we not wondered whether two persons who disagree had actually seen the same film or read the same book!

The aim of criticism is modest because, even in the ideal case, it only helps us to appreciate a work of art by inducing us to refocus our attention on it. (Many of us need such help in connection with *some* works of art.) The critic helps us to see in the work of art what makes it worthy of consideration. All he need do is begin the process which we, of our own accord, can continue. He need not finish it. (Perhaps he cannot.) And he cer-

6

tainly does not have to duplicate the work of art in a verbal medium, assuming that he can do so.

A great deal is expected of the critic. He must know how to describe in an intelligible, interesting manner his various internal states. Not everyone has the ability to do this. But the critic who has this accomplishment must respond in great measure to works of art and be aware of his responses. He must be peculiarly adept at noticing them, of being able to compare present with past experiences and to assess their adequacy. There is a skill in being able to organize one's awarenesses, to muster them together into a dialectically interesting, coherent pattern. It is hard to believe that this process can be performed "unconsciously." In order to be able to respond fruitfully, one must have a rich background of experiences. And this background may involve a wide range of material: historical knowledge, biographical facts, sociological and psychological hypotheses. In criticizing, one wants to bring a new experience to someone else; and for this act of persuasion, it is difficult to say beforehand what might do the trick of making one "see" the work of art. Of course, the critic himself initially must have responded to the work of art deeply, fully. In the ideal case, he must see all that there is in the work of art — even more than the artist himself perceived. For he must be conscious and take note of his perception of what he sees. This the artist himself may not achieve. (However, it is not necessary that the critic be able to create the work of art, too. Critics, so far as they function as such, are responding to a pre-existent object or an event, whose occurrence does not depend on them. Artists, except for their reliance on the tradition within which they work and their experience of life, create ex nihilo or afresh.) An artist should be critical of his work, of course, but his act of criticism, like his act of creation, may be spontaneous and subliminal. For a critic to respond in such a way is to abdicate his post. An artist often fails to see inconsistencies in his work or to detect unconscious meanings that are clearly there. A critic who misses them is not much worth his salt. And he is not likely to be an effective critic if he is not at least in partial control of his unconscious responses to works of art.

A critic talks, and we, the listeners watch the critic *and* the work of art. How does he give us the insight? His act is not unlike that of the conjurer. The critic speaks and gestures and dances: he literally charms us into seeing what he sees the work

7

of art to be. He describes the work and evokes all manner of information to reveal to us the essence of it. Thus, his act is also one of revelation. He does not prove in any deductive manner; he cannot demonstrate his conclusion — but he can show us what is there. Like Socrates' torpedo fish, he bewitches us into perceiving.[1] Bewitching? Charming? The activity is not as occult or as mysterious as those terms suggest; but there is nothing mechanical or automatic in the process. There is a knack and a skill involved. The logic — for there is a logic here — is very complicated; and these complications all hinge on the nature of art, the kind of seeing and enjoying appropriate to works of art, and the kind of evaluation that is appropriate to works of art.

If criticism itself is talking, then it is funded on a transaction with the work of art, and so it is a "seeing." The whole is like divination.

2　STYLES OF CRITICISM: THE LARGER DESIGN

There are many ways of treating works of art, but not all of them are relevant to aesthetics. Works of art may appear in a history of technology, as accounts and pictures of buildings, bridges, household utensils and machines often do. When folk tales, poems, stories, paintings and drawings function as source material for the delineation of the ideas and values of a society (as they do in Burckhardt's studies of the Renaissance in Italy or Huizinga's studies of Gothic Europe), it is not essentially significant that the items examined are works of art. Any other set of objects would serve as well. We can be fascinated by archaeological finds or with the reconstructions of medieval music. The age of an object, because of the corrosive effect of time, adds an interest to it. But its worth as a work of art is another thing. Even in the history of an art form — as in the history of the Italian sonnet, English prose in the seventeenth century or the development of landscape painting — the treatment is not purely aesthetic. It is true that we have the history of an art (notice how the word "art" shifts its meaning), but the narrative must take into account all relevant examples: and the relevance of an example is not always related to the aesthetic success or value of the item. Although the history of pottery in Ancient Egypt or the history of medieval Latin grammar could both conceivably be written solely from the viewpoint of technique, the history of the sonnet or landscape painting would not even be attempted except for their value as art. The history of the fugue, an account of Shakespeare's prosody, the history of perspective in painting are all borderline cases. Such histories could be written neutrally; the discussion of these subjects does not have to deal with them as works of art. To take another example, the interest of an object may be clearly parasitic on the fact that it is a work of art. But we must not confuse such parasitic interests with aesthetic ones. Paintings can become news and appear in newspaper headlines because they are works of art. High auction prices and riots at premieres of musical performances are such news. They would not have any snob appeal (and thus function in advertising appeals) if they were not works of art. As candidates for future greatness, they become objects of investment and acquire economic value. But considerations of scarcity aside, the values of the old masters are by no means bestowed by their age. This is true even of religious art: paintings and frescoes would not be made, nor music composed as integral parts of religious life, except that these objects are beautiful. There would probably be little merit in the dedication of a mural to the Holy Virgin if it were not both beautiful and pious.

How must we treat objects as art? The purpose of this study is to formulate an answer. At present I begin with samples of criticisms that are not obviously nonaesthetic. These may be roughly divided into three kinds: the critic may describe his responses to the work of art; he may discuss the motives and causal conditions that impinge on the work of art; or he may describe the rhetoric of the work of art. No piece of critical writing will belong wholly to any one of the three categories; it will obviously be an admixture. But usually one of them will predominate. What is more important is that critical fashion tends to favor one form over the others from time to time.

I

Many works of art require interpretation. Simply, in themselves, they may be difficult, problematic, leaving us with the feeling that we have only partially understood them. They may even leave us in doubt as to whether we are on the right approach. At such times, we want to be able to compare our own impressions and responses with those of another person. In a crude fashion, we frequently ask someone else "How do you feel about it?" Do you like it?" "Did you enjoy it?" And what is worse, we cannot always tell what our responses were. We may not be in a position to say whether we liked or did not like the work of art. We may not be able to call our responses a feeling, though response there was. But we commonly believe that a work of art is an expression and that some sort of attitudinal response is required, for human agents are involved in the phenomenon of art.

One mode of criticism has traditionally been called impressionistic, and though it is an unfortunate name, I retain it here since it is well-established. The impressionistic critics correctly assume that what is important (and helpful to have available for the record) in the study of art is a full, evocative and expressive response to a work of art. The emphasis in the criticism falls on describing the critic's responses. Thus, impressionistic criticism is based on the belief that a critic is one who as a result of special training and a special capacity, is capable of this full response. This criticism further presupposes that some responses are more interesting than others, that it is possible to distinguish full, adequate responses from partial, defective ones. The critic is further required to have the capacity for communicating his response, of evoking it and of reproducing it in others. One method by which the critic may achieve this effect is impressionistic writing: impressionistic is two senses; one which reports the impressions received by the critic and which tries to create an impression, occasionally running to full, colorful, poetic writing. The chief purpose of criticism is to convey to the reader or listener the full flavor and nuance of the experience that he (the critic) had on studying, viewing, contemplating, scanning a work of art. To this end, he uses everything at his disposal: all the resources of language. He emphasizes and verbally gestures; in rich evocative language, layer on layer, he pieces together various impressions until a pattern is formed. Into this pattern may go historical facts and historical reconstructions, literary and technical information, biographical sidelights — anything that conceivably might evoke in the reader the response that approaches in quality his response to the work of art. There is a high verbal skill involved: and it is in this sense that criticism (and particularly impressionistic criticism) was thought to be an art.

Unless the re-creation of impression is possible, this sort of criticism is, of course, impossible. That a number of persons can share similar impressions in this way is a necessary presupposition of impressionistic criticism. A famous example of such criticism we may find in the writings of Walter Pater on Renaissance art and literature. In his essay on Botticelli, discussing the *Birth of Venus,* he calmly describes the effect of the painting: and he does this by sticking relatively closely to the picture itself.

> . . . a picture . . . of Venus rising from the sea, in which the
> grotesque emblems of the middle age, and a landscape full of
> its peculiar feeling, and even its strange draperies, powdered
> all over in the Gothic manner with a quaint conceit of daisies,
> frame a figure that reminds you of the faultless nude studies
> of Ingres. At first, perhaps, you are attracted only by a quaint-
> ness of design, which seems to recall all at once whatever you
> have read of Florence in the fifteenth century; afterwards you
> may think that this quaintness must be incongruous with the
> subject, and that the colour is cadaverous or at least cold.[1]

He goes on. Is it helpful? Sometimes it is. In the essay on da
Vinci, there are passages of historical evocation which run into
biographical sketches. "The science of that age was all divination,
clairvoyance, unsubjected to our exact modern formulas, seeking
in an instant of vision to concentrate a thousand experiences."[2]
These statements serve as setting for the discussion of individual
works by da Vinci. He says of the so-called *Saint John the Baptist*
of the Louvre that it is "one of the few naked figures Leonardo
painted — whose delicate brown flesh and woman's hair no one
would go out in the wilderness to seek, and whose treacherous
smile would have us understand something far beyond the outward gesture or circumstance."[3] The essay moves to its climax
in the passage on the Mona Lisa, which begins affirmatively
enough: "La Gioconda is, in the truest sense, Leonardo's masterpiece, the revealing instance of his mode of thought and work.
In suggestiveness, only the *Melancholia* of Dürer is comparable
to it . . ." and builds up to a crescendo which has been for many
years the despair of scientific critics.

> Hers is the head upon which all "the ends of the world are come,"
> and the eyelids are a little weary. It is a beauty wrought out
> from within upon the flesh, the deposit, little cell by cell, of
> strange thoughts and fantastic reveries and exquisite passions . . . .
> All the thoughts and experience of the world have etched and
> moulded there, in that which they have of power to refine and
> make expressive the outward form, the animalism of Greece, the
> lust of Rome, the mysticism of the middle age with its spiritual
> ambition and imaginative loves, the return of the Pagan world,
> the sins of the Borgias. She is older than the rocks among which
> she sits; like the vampire, she has been dead many times, and
> learned the secrets of the grave; and has been a diver in deep seas,
> and keeps their fallen day about her; and trafficked for strange
> webs with Eastern merchants: and, as Leda, was the mother of
> Helen of Troy, and, as Saint Anne, the mother of Mary; and all
> this has been to her but as the sound of lyres and flutes, and

lives only in the delicacy with which it has moulded the changing
lineaments, and tinged the eyelids and the hands.[4]

It is certainly clear that for Pater she is the eternal feminine. But
in criticism, what has this passage achieved?

Pater is describing the impression he receives from the painting.
The *Mona Lisa* reminds him of something "older than the rocks
among which she sits"; of something like the vampire that "has
been dead many times, and learned the secrets of the grave."
She "has been a diver in deep seas, and keeps their fallen day
about her; and trafficked for strange webs with Eastern mer-
chants." This is fancy writing: and it does not surprise us that
the name of Leda, the mother of Helen of Troy, and of St. Anne,
the mother of Mary, naturally occur to Pater as further associations. But then nothing is to Pater's mind like the *Mona Lisa.*
The passage is hot and wild, and for the average reader who is
interested in discovering what he ought to see in the paintings
of da Vinci, Pater's reports would seem excessive and idiosyncratic. But there is nothing wrong with the method itself. If
anything has gone askew, it is the heat of the writing that defeats
the purposes at hand. Much of what Pater writes is so extraordinary that we become interested in Pater himself. It must
be noticed that we can mistrust some impressionistic critics (like
Pater) because we can readily select those reports that are
within the range of the reasonable and those clearly beyond the
range. It is sometimes difficult to tell whether we are being
influenced by the prose description or by the work to which the
description applies. In Pater, the writing itself acquires an autonomy, magnetizing our attention to itself, whereas, properly, it
should be significant yet dependent on the work; i.e., comprehensible in itself but humbly deferential to the work in question.
Here impressionistic criticism is at fault, because impressionism
has gone wild. It needs to be curbed. Thus, the presupposition of
impressionistic criticism is fair enough. Examples of it could
be multiplied; but it is obvious without doing so, that the effects of
music, poetry, cityscapes, even prose may be rendered impres-
sionistically.

II

The basic presupposition of contextual criticism is that the
condition of the act of creation is important: particularly the

"consideration of the irrational underlying predicament of the artist himself."[5] Any discussion of the causal contexts begins with the works of art, of course; for otherwise it would not be art criticism. But a complete analysis requires a larger context, and the critic readily supplies this from a number of sources. In the abstract, they may be called the conditions of the work of art; and this includes not only the specific causes that give rise to the work in question and which are reflected in it (like the insanity of Van Gogh, the Oedipus complex of Dostoievsky) but also the characteristics of a culture that appear in it. Any work of art makes evident the spirit of the times, the unconscious motives and values of the society and its components. The work of art reveals, or more strongly, *betrays* these unconscious motives in a wider sense.

A large portion of contextual criticism consists of biographical and sociological analyses of works of art. Either type presupposes that the facts brought to the criticism are relevant to it because they materially influence the form of the work of art and may be seen in the form that the work of art assumes. (The most familiar examples are Freudian, Marxist, or religious analyses of both artists and works of art.) If these factors influence the creation of the work of art, then one ought to be able to turn it around and say that, from looking at the work of art, you can discover these factors. And here you have the logic of motivational criticism.

When a work of art is difficult and it resists our attempt to understand it, we may ask, why is it the way it is? And localizing our reference further, we may ask, why is a characteristic of the work the way it is? (Why are the watches in the painting limp and drooping over the edge of the table? Why do the events of the novel all take place at night?) And it is not unusual at all for these questions to be answered by referring to what the artist intended, or in terms of its connection with the spirit of the times and the mores of a society. It is difficult not to answer these questions by reference to some causal factors. Thus we may explain the surrealist features of a painting in terms of modern science, the realism readily achieved by the use of the camera, and the need to delve beneath the visible surface of things. It makes sense to explain the smile of a Mona Lisa (so while it was originally a joke, it is no longer wholly a joke) by saying that it was the smugness of a woman who is about to announce her pregnancy for the first time. Another art historian has accounted, half in jest, for the elongation of the human forms in El Greco's works by his astigmatism. Though it is a dogma in aesthetics that all intentional, motivational, causal studies of works of art are extraaesthetic, it is not obvious that such analyses are completely irrelevant, for it cannot be denied that there are various causal conditions underlying works of art; and many of them, were we to understand them, would be illuminating (perhaps not of the works immediately but certainly of the circumstances surrounding the genesis of the work).[6]

"You *must* look through the surface of American art and see the inner diabolism of the symbolic meaning. Otherwise it is all mere childishness."[7] This is said by D. H. Lawrence in the course of discussing Hawthorne's *The Scarlet Letter*. We must, according to him, discover the symbolic meanings of any work of art. How is this done? In his rambunctious manner (the usual mask that Lawrence wears in essay writing), he suggests how at the beginning of his studies.

> Art-speech is the only truth. An artist is usually a damned liar, but his art, if it be art, will tell you the truth of his day. And that is all that matters. . . .
> The old American artists were hopeless liars. But they were artists, in spite of themselves. Which is more than you can say of most living practitioners.
> And you can please yourself, when you read *The Scarlet Letter,* whether you accept what that sugary, blue-eyed little darling of a Hawthorne has to say for himself, false as all darlings are, or whether you read the impeccable truth of his art-speech.[8]

The truth contained in "art-speech" (an ugly phrase) is apparently not the surface meaning of what is said. We must garner the truth by taking the artist by surprise. We cannot take his expressed intention at face value; neither what he says nor what he claims he means to say.

> The curious thing about art-speech is that it prevaricates so terribly, I mean it tells such lies. I suppose because we always all the time tell ourselves lies. And out of a pattern of lies art weaves the truth. Like Dostoevsky posing as a sort of Jesus, but most truthfully revealing himself all the while as a little horror . . . .
> The artist usually sets out — or used to — to point a moral and adorn a tale. The tale, however, points the other way, as a rule. Two blankly opposing morals, the artist's and the tale's. Never trust the artist. Trust the tale. The proper function of a critic is to save the tale from the artist who created it.[9]

15

From the viewpoint of aesthetic orthodoxy, what Lawrence says is safe enough. He is going to pay attention to the work. But when he discusses the work itself, he supplies a context — his theory of the whole man — that which incorporates and fulfills "it": "it being the deepest *whole* self of man, the self in its wholeness, not idealistic halfness."[10]   Lawrence's main interest lies "much lower than personality . . . [in the] swirls of conflicting impulses and emotions."[11]   Therefore, it is not at all surprising to discover him discussing Melville and his *Typee* in terms of the unconscious psyche of Melville; and Melville's predicament in terms of the "American Dream."

> Melville at his best invariably wrote from a sort of dream-self, so that events which he relates as actual fact have indeed a far deeper reference to his own soul, his own inner life.
> So in *Typee* when he tells of his entry into the valley of the dread cannibals of Nukuheva. Down this narrow, steep, horrible dark gorge he slides and struggles as we struggle in a dream, or in the act of birth, to emerge in the green Eden of the Golden Age, the valley of the cannibal savages. This is a bit of birth-myth, of re-birth myth, on Melville's part — unconscious, no doubt, because his running underconsciousness was always mystical and symbolical. He wasn't aware that he was being mystical.[12]
> There on the island, where the golden-green great palmtrees chinked in the sun, and the elegant reed houses let the sea-breeze through, and the people went naked and laughed a great deal, and Fayaway put flowers in his hair for him — great red hibiscus flowers, and frangipani — O God, why wasn't he happy? Why wasn't he?
> Because he wasn't.
> Well, it's hard to make a man happy.
> But I should not have been happy either. One's soul seems under a vacuum, in the South Seas.
> The truth of the matter is, one cannot go back. Some men can: renegade. But Melville couldn't go back: and Gauguin couldn't really go back: and I know now that I could never go back. Back towards the past, savage life. One cannot go back. It is one's destiny inside one.[13]

This is enough to indicate what is involved in contextual criticism. That it can be fascinating and helpful in our understanding of a work of art need not be further emphasized. The usefulness of such criticism is wholly to be gauged by how much it advances the comprehension of the work of art. And since works of art are in significant ways different from other things in the world, they would be illuminated (one would assume) in ways different from other things. So the strangeness of Lawrence's discoveries should not, in itself, surprise us, nor count against them. But clearly the degree to which we can admit the relevance and can sympathize with the context supplied would have a bearing on the utility of Lawrence's motivational criticism. How reputable is Lawrence's theory of the whole man? Or when we are confronted by a Marxist analysis of art, to what extent do we agree with the economic analysis of the condition of art? In discussing the trends in contemporary paintings, Herbert Read writes:

> . . . the cabinet picture has lost, or is quickly losing, all economic justification, and to try to keep it alive by State patronage is like trying to keep the dodo alive in a zoo. Indeed, there is more than a fanciful parallel between the museum and the zoo; they are both places where we keep rare and eccentric specimens at public expense. And why not, to be logical, put the artist himself in the zoo: let him have a comfortable cage with a northern light, and there let him produce obsolete art objects to be hung in an aquarium-like building next door.[14]

"Cabinet painting is a defunct art, perpetuated by defunct institutions." The comments are about a class of objects; but these remarks would be relevant to one's study of particular works. And one's interpretation of a modern painting is bound to be influenced by whether one agrees with Read or not and particularly whether cabinet painting, as such, is a natural product of a certain socio-economic form of life.

III

It should be obvious by now that the main difficulties of both impressionistic as well as contextual criticism is that they can both easily become irrelevant. The former becomes an independent entity in itself. The latter becomes a historical, economic, biographical or socio-psychological treatise. But when we think of works of art, we would agree with the poet who said "A poem should not mean/But be."[15] One can, nevertheless, still ask, what *can* one do with something which simply *is?* Describe it? Analyze it? We would say we must treat it for what it is. But to say so is not to supply much of a guide. We dogmatically say that this statement presupposes the independence of the object from its surroundings — its causal origins, its utilitarian consequences or its social ramifications. Yet the work *in itself* may embody religious and moral significances, and reflect the society that produced it. The critic may still try to describe the work as an entity on its

17

own (that is as an object, ergo objectively); so he can begin by delineating its parts as well as the form, gently touching on its emotional effects, or the tradition that lies behind it. Primarily he would try to stick to the text, the score, the canvas. For to bring in anything else would be to introduce something conjectural, hypothetical; and the entire discourse would end in a "mere interpretation," probably a purely subjective one. In the most extreme form of such criticism, a work of art — for example a piece of sculpture, perhaps a figure of a woman — would be analyzed without mention of representational parts (head, torso, hem of the dress, etc.). The critic abstemiously describes the object simply in terms of abstract shapes, measurements, configurations, etc. Such a restricted method results in criticism that seems very dry. If a man (say a saint) is represented in a painting, it seems silly not to name the configuration as such. But most "objective criticism" is not so self-denying. One might call this mode of criticism rhetorical — but in doing so, we must remember that the idea of rhetoric first applies to the form and structure of discourse. The relevant idea of form involved here includes not only the structure but also the appropriateness of the subject matter to the form and all of these in the dynamic context of its effect on the viewer. (Alternative names might have been formal criticism, stylistic criticism, or structural criticism.)

In the most austere cases, rhetorical criticism approaches the condition of a catalogue itemization.

> SAINT JEROME IN HIS STUDY
> *Physical data*: Oak, 81/16 x 5¼ in. (20.5 x 13.3 cm.) (total surface). Transferred to a new panel in 1956. The presence of various layers under the ground, including one of lead minium, gives strong indication of a previous transfer. The date 1442 is painted at the upper left between the back of the chair and the curtain. Text of the letter placed on the table, written in minuscule Gothic letters: *Reuerendissimo in Christo patri* . . . Pentimenti: the astrolabe, the fingers of the Saint's right hand, and the cushion on the chair.[16]

This example from an actual exhibition catalogue is indeed staid and sober. A more amusing, but no less mathematical, example occurs in Giorgio Vasari's discussion of Michelangelo's design of the tribunal of St. Peter's.

> My description may help the faithful executors to understand the master's intention and bridle the desire of the malignant to change it, while it will instruct and delight the choice spirits who

18

love this art. The model provides for a span of one hundred and eighty-six palms from wall to wall across the great tribune over the great surrounding cornice, which rests on four large double pilasters with carved Corinthian capitals, decorated with architrave, frieze and cornice. . . . At the place where the cupola springs from the tribune is a base of travertine with a way 6 palms broad, going round, 33 palms 11 inches across, and 11 palms 10 inches high to the cornice. The cornice above is about 8 palms, and the projection 6½ palms. [17]

Some of the arts lend themselves more easily to descriptions of this sort than others. It may be that music, ceramics, perhaps nonobjective paintings are best treated in this way, a mixture of technical and formal analysis. But there are examples of rigorous formal analyses in representational painting and literature also. They are numerous, thanks to the activities of the "New Critics." I take an example from William Empson's *Seven Types of Ambiguity*.

There is another Shakespearean negative in one of the songs of Ophelia, an irrelevant little word in itself, which supports a faint but an elaborate reverberation of feeling; becomes, to an attent ear, a full ambiguity; and drapes itself for a moment over the whole structure of the play.

Oph: *White his Shrow'd as the Mountain Snow.*
Que: Alas looke heere my Lord.
Oph: *Larded with sweet flowers:*
Which bewept to the grave did not go,
With true-love showres. (*Hamlet,* IV, v.) [18]

Empson is arrested by the unexpected negative in Ophelia's song. What can it mean in the context of this scene? And what permeating influence could it have? (In his iconographic studies, Irwin Panofsky asks similar questions about mottos and emblems that occur in paintings, particularly of the Baroque period. His answers as a whole relate to the paintings under discussion, but his essays are contributions to the history of ideas and thus belong more properly to contextual criticism.) [19]

Here is Empson in operation, ingenious and startling.

Not may negate *going* or *weeping*. That the ear expects *did go* may mean that all nature wept for Polonius; . . . that it gets *did not go* may mean that, whether Hamlet wept for him or not, he went first into the lobby where he was *safely stowed;* that it expects *did go* may mean that Hamlet is dead to her, that she feels he must really be dead and she ought to weep for him, and that he *is going* to England at the risk of his life; that it gets

19

did not go may mean that he is not really dead, that she must not weep for one who is alive and has so wronged her (the end of their love was not his death but his murder of her father), and that he is *going* to come back from England safely. She may alter the song through an echo of the misanthropy of her lover, from a feeling that *flowers* ought not to be mixed up with corpses, that the plucked flowers are the objects on a bier that ought really to be mourned for, though they are *not*. Or the dead man of the song may be Hamlet's father, so that the whole scene is a sort of satire against the Queen. I must consider the whole scene to insist upon this point.[20]

And Empson does go on to consider the whole scene. But we may well ask, why suppose this method of grammatical and formal analysis would succeed at all? And if it did, what would it achieve? The answers given are purist at heart. A work of art must be taken on its own. All the parts must be relevant to each other. They must stand for a single order. In very complicated works (like *Hamlet*) this unity is frequently threatened by the very complexity of the work. But a scheme must be there, if it is a successful work of art, that underpins and girds the whole structure and rhetoric of the work; and we must try to discover it, for that is exactly where we may locate the essential meaning of a work of art. In principle one may begin anywhere, for a work of art is a unity and all the parts contained in it contribute to the meaning of the work. Empson had discovered that the presence of an ambiguity or an irony (which radiates out and permeates the surrounding texture) was one useful way to show the nature of the forces that held the work together.[21] The scheme, he would claim, arises out of the core of the work of art; but wherever one begins, the end results must be the same.

But it might still be asked: if a work of art must simply be, why must we tamper with it and subject it to analysis? The answer is complicated. First, we must reply that sometimes there are occasions when we must take the poetry and the music as pure sounds, just as we often take human beings on pure looks; and if this is what we want, then the analysis probably will impede us. But from the sound, we often want to move on to its meaning, just as, with people we know, we want to move on from their personal looks to an understanding of their character. And these critics were trying to supply just such diagnostic understanding in their work of criticism.[22] In order to do this, the critic must have at his disposal a fair amount of equilibrium and very strong defenses. For he must have the power to react to the poem (or the work of art) "strongly and definitely" and further be able to hold on to this reaction as in a snap shot, so that he can scrutinize it without letting his past reactions interfere. (This takes a firm mind.) Ultimately, we pursue the analysis of our reaction to a work of art in order to see why we have reacted in a particular manner. The poem, therefore, becomes revealing of our inner states. What we then discover may surprise us — just as what we initially find to be attractive in some people may turn out to be not very reputable. Perhaps not all works of art can survive such analyses — and these may even include some good works, because after our scrutiny we may never have the fresh, enthralled first reaction again. But at least we know that we once had such a reaction. What we want to be able to say after an act of scrutiny is "This is all right. I have the right feeling about this. I know the way it is meant to affect me." Not "This is beautiful because I like it" or "This is beautiful for the following theoretical reasons." Since the act of scrutiny involves the total reaction of the critic, it is to be expected that some descriptions of the emotional responses of the observer be included in formalist criticism. But being purists, formalist critics try (as much as possible) to leave out "non-aesthetic" considerations and to keep their discussions prosaic and dry. All of this is naturally to be expected of the formalists.

IV

There are probably other patterns of criticisms. But the afore-mentioned constitute the main divisions. They do not usually occur as pure specimens, though there are many examples that are near the pure state. D. F. Tovey's measure by measure tonal analysis of Beethoven's pianoforte sonatas is a prime example of rhetorical analysis. [23] Even in the samples I have chosen to illustrate my categories, there are "impurities." D. H. Lawrence is impressionistic in part when he discusses *Moby Dick,* and he quotes copiously (a trait more typical of the formalists). And Empson's storehouse of semantic theory, social linguistics, etc., relies heavily on the historical sciences. In practice, the three modes are inextricably mixed: we depend on tradition and exper-ience to give us clues on how to interpret what we see in the work, whether in part or as a whole. Ultimately we cannot avoid being impressionistic to some extent, for the very analysis is worth performing because art as emotional expression is what interests us.

If there is any mode that needs emphasizing at all, it is impressionistic criticism. Works of art are difficult to talk about: in subtle, frustrating ways, they resist classification and label. The nature of language does not make it particularly easy to name, describe, anatomize our affective, impressionistic responses to works of art. Yet when we see a painting, when we hear a piece of music, it is our immediate responses to it — presymbolic and verbally unmediated — the responses of our emotions and our visceral selves that we find significant.

When I experience a work of art, I know how I respond to it all right; nevertheless, I want to know whether or not my emotional response is like someone else's. It would be valuable, and therapeutic as well, to have a whole corpus of impressionistic reports about how various persons have responded to a work of art — more prosaic versions of "On First Looking into Chapman's Homer," or "On Hearing a Symphony of Beethoven." We might possibly discover that many people react as we do. We might also learn that, in large measure, we all react subjectively to works of art (and thus begin to realize to what extent we live cannibalistically on them and use them as jumping off points of reverie). Where the impressionistic report is a sober, responsible one, we would notice what our emotional psyches gain from our trafficking with works of art: and thereby come that much closer to an account of the nature of art.

Criticism, like analysis is a communal activity. We do not write critical essays merely for ourselves or talk merely to ourselves in viewing works of art. But in writing criticism, we first of all make clear to ourselves what we see and how and why we see it so. Secondly, we attempt to make public (and therefore responsible) what we feel, how we respond to the work of art. Insight, accuracy and responsibility need to be balanced. But most of all, criticism needs to be bold — bold in its insights as well as its errors. In point of fact, we learn much from our mistakes and our overstatements, for in recognizing them as such, we have come to a more just view. Time and repeated effort will usually correct our mistakes. But if we are not courageous (and sometimes daring), the brave insights will never come forth. Thus it is the startling (perhaps courageous) views that we need most of all. If the critic's assertion is mere exaggeration, it will eventually die. But it may also turn out to be the source of much future insight.

22

II | THE LOGIC OF AESTHETIC JUDGMENTS

3 | THE DETAILS OF CRITICISM: ANALYSIS AND INTERPRETATION

Many types of assertions can be made about a work of art. Therefore, criticism is ambiguous in function. When we criticize, we comment, we analyze; and the comments may be neutral. But they need not be; and the trend of the discussion may be either favorable, unfavorable or a neutral mixture of the two. If there is a summation, the criticism ends in a value judgment. In all of this procedure, we are in the habit of drawing a sharp distinction between analysis and description, on the one hand, and evaluation and praise, on the other. But there is a third class of activity that seems to be a combination of both: appreciation, recognition, enjoyment. For example, a man who appreciates a Bach fugue understands it and recognizes its value for what it is; and we think of enjoyment as *liking* enriched by a comprehension.

Analyzing	Inspecting	Liking
Describing	Appreciating	Taking pleasure
Scrutinizing	Grading	Praising
Interpreting	Assessing	Lauding
Contemplating	Estimating	Emoting
Scanning	Enjoying[1]	Attitudinizing
Viewing	Criticizing	
Studying	Evaluating	
Inspecting		

Critics typically discuss a work of art in a detailed, particularized way as well as offering more general comments about the work in relation to the life of the artist, his other works, or the times in which it was created. Analysis and Synthesis are the words we use for these two methods. The two are clearly related. There is security in criticism that is grounded on an analysis of a work of art. Analysis here means dissection — an anatomization of the work. We feel that somehow this particularization gives the critic a command over the material. The synoptic view formed by a critic may be most arresting and brilliant, but if he seems not to know the details of the works he is discussing, we lose confidence in his views. The synthesized, over-all view is as important as the detailed analysis of the work; and, furthermore, we expect the former to be grounded on the latter. Though we tend to think that the results of analysis is more dependable and solid than those of synthesis, it is still possible to evaluate the larger synthetic view as sound or unsound, just as it is possible to judge the analysis of the details as correct or incorrect.

It is not easy to give a simple definition of analysis. It is true that we avoid broad general descriptions — those which indicate the far-reaching influences of the work or its deep spiritual significances, redolent with the movement of the *Zeitgeist* — in giving an analysis. In the following example, what Virgil Thomson says is plausible: but one would be hesitant to say that the passage is analytical.

> The despair in his [Bartok] quartets is no mere personal maladjustment. It is a realistic facing, through the medium of pure feeling, of the human condition, the state of man as a moral animal, as this was perceptible to a musician of high moral sensibilities living in Hungary.
>
> No other musician of our century has faced its horrors quite so frankly, so unassumingly, so squarely. The quartets of Bartok have a sincerity, indeed, and a natural elevation that are wellnigh unique in the history of music. . . . His music approached more and more a state of systematic discord, rendered more and more truly and convincingly the state of European man in his time. His six string quartets are the cream of Bartok's repertory, the essence of his deepest thought and feeling, his most powerful and humane communication.[2]

But the chief barrier to giving a simple account of analysis consists in the complex, multiform nature of analysis itself. Many different processes go under this one name.

1) Identifications: One gives (when known) the name of the artist, title of the work, date of creation, and, where possible, its location. "The noblest sea that Turner ever painted, and, if so, the noblest certainly ever painted by man, is that of the Slave Ship, the chief Academy picture of the exhibition of 1840 [now in the Boston Museum of Art.]"[3] "*Agon,* a ballet composed by Igor Stravinsky in his personal twelve tone style, choreographed by George Balanchine, and danced by the New York City Ballet was [first performed on November 27, 1957.]"[4] So important is the authorship that the existence of an artist is often hyposthesized on the basis of similarities noticed in anonymous works. There are artists like "The Master of the Virgo inter Virgines," "The Achilles-painter" (a worker of Greek vases), who are known by the name of their chief works and who are otherwise unknown, though sometimes the place and time of their activity are postulated on stylistic grounds.

2) We make further identifications by mentioning the media used: that the work is a painting on canvas; a drawing on rice paper using brush and ink; a mural; a collage of paper, burlap, and rattan chair seat; a poem in middle English; a composition for piano and voice, or for orchestra composed of strings and percussion.

3) The form (or organization scheme) is also indicated: it is a symphony, a triptych, an epic poem, a sonnet, etc. It is not always easy to differentiate the media employed from the conventional form of the work. The mention of classical Greek pottery (a kalyx, for example) seems to cover both the medium and the form, as does the identification of a prose work as an epistolary novel. Sometimes the organization of the work is matter for demonstration. Then it is not something that can be named but something that must be described. (See below, 6.)

4) Further identification of "form" is made by pointing out the subject matter: that the work is a portrait or a still life; a nature poem or a love sonnet; a tone poem; a comedy of manners or a revenge tragedy; a western film. In this sense, the subject is general and usually identified with *form*: for portraiture as a form can be particularized into the content. (See below, 9) The items that I have separated here as 2, 3 and 4 fuse into each other readily. This is symptomized by the fact that the term "form" can refer to any one of these three.

5) One can also mention various technical features of the work: that the music employs the twelve-tone system; that the

ballet is in the classical style of Bournonville; that the painting is an example of pointillism, the mural, a fresco; the novel, a stream of consciousness novel. Sometimes these features are called "form" also, but the application of this term here is not wholly unambiguous.

Though the points brought out in the five preceding paragraphs figure in all analyses, they are, strictly speaking, preliminaries to analysis; and usually they do not occupy much time or space. They are only incidental. Unless the very authorship of the work or the very classification of the work ("this is only a detective story") crucially makes a difference in the way we go about discussing it, we simply mention such features and proceed with the main job of analysis which consists of a dissection of the work.

6) This analysis consists in the discussion of the features of the work of art. Here again, there are several levels on which we proceed. (A) We may mention various physical features: size, color, shape, the way the pigment is applied to the canvas; the meter, beat, accent, timbre and how the instrumental colors are used in a musical composition; the physical measurements (the whole and parts) of a building, its material, engineering features, etc. The dissection may be very minute, a point-by-point, moment-by-moment discussion of the work. In the analysis of a poem, for example, the procedure would involve concentration on the words used, their juxtapositions, the rhyme scheme, the rhythmic flow, the rise and fall of accent, tone and tensional patterns, etc. In a musical analysis, the tonality and harmonic schemes, the thematic organization of melodies and motifs, the orchestration, etc. (B) At the same time, we may describe the characteristics of the work as a whole. This is done usually by discussing the stylistic features of the work. "The landscape is reduced to a system of rectilinear forms seen at right angles to the picture plane . . ." "The details and organization of the work are simple, abstract, and well-balanced — it is very Apollonian in feeling." "The tonality of the work is predominantly dark, somber and inward." "When the figure is draped, the Baroque idea becomes particularly evident. The artists seek voluminous and massive garments which under the stress of an emphatic pose take heavy folds passing in a single diagonal sweep from top to bottom of the whole figure."[5]

7) A particularly useful way of characterizing a work may be called the "mood-features" method, for want of a better label.

This characterization involves a description of the mood of the work as a whole. "In the 'Pieta' a more epic conception is realized, for the impression conveyed is of a universal and cosmic disaster: the air is rent with the shrieks of desperate angels whose bodies are contorted in a raging frenzy of compassion."[6] "Claude's world is not to be lived in, only to be looked at in a mood of pleasing melancholy or suave reverie."[7] "There is[in Mozart] a profoundly disturbing melancholy. . . . It is a still, unplumbed melancholy underlying even his brightest, and most vivacious movements."[8] "In the third movement [of Op. 76, no. 2, Haydn] reverts to the octave-doubling of his youth, but this time to produce a masterpiece of weird effectiveness, the famous canonic 'Witches' Minuet.' "[9] Melancholy, eerie, weird, desperate: these are features of the work of art, there on the surface of the work or down below to be plumbed — but they are also inner-states of the observer (or better yet, the result of his discrimination and sensitivity).

8) The sixth and seventh categories above need to be divided in another way. Many of the features that we point out in a work of art are straightforward, nonaesthetic properties: large, thin, orange-colored, rough-surfaced, squarish, loud, rapid-paced, an E-flat tone on the oboe. "The long thin figures, the repetition of perpendicular lines, . . . the long masks, too big in proportion for the heads . . ."[10] Such phrases function as verbal indices, pointing out visible features in the work of art. Quotations in the analysis of poetry and music serve much the same function. Thus, the critic may say "The two bars quoted in example No. 1 are the whole of the first theme. The second bar is echoed softly an octave higher."[11] "The time changes from triple to duple; instead of runs, arpeggios, and the skips, we have smooth cantabile outlines."[12]

Along with these regular properties, however, we find the occurrence of what we must call, for want of a better name, aesthetic properties.[13] Dynamic tension, dramatic sweep; nervous kinesthetic lines; lively shapes, full of humor; harmonious blending of warm and cool colors; monumental effect; tragic climax; not tragic but pathetic; sentimental — these are examples. They crop up in critical discourse, intermixed with nonaesthetic properties, and they obviously depend on each other. Aesthetic and nonaesthetic properties are alike in many ways. (i) They are both objective, veridical properties of entities — works of art as well as everyday things. That two occurrences of a color are instances of redness is seen, just as much as the fact that one is warmer than the other in tone. A line in a drawing may be hard, thin, long, dark and curved. We *see* that: but we also *see* that it is nervous and uncertain. And warm colors and cool, nervous lines and flabby ones occur in contexts that are not artistic as well as in works of art. (ii) Both properties may be treated in similar ways. We can *say* that a line is dark and long, and we can also *say* that it is nervous; so that the line may be described to be long and dark as well as nervous. (iii) In many instances, we must learn to see both of these kinds of features and learn the language for describing them. In the process of learning them, we can make mistakes or misdescribe what we correctly see. And such mistakes can be corrected. The judgments we make about them are corrigible.

But the differences between the two kinds of properties are more important. (i) For one thing, about aesthetic properties there is frequently a wide difference of opinion, and the validation of the two kinds of properties proceed in different ways. [14] If there is a question about the color of an object, we can look again, check on a color chart, etc. If we did not think that the harmonic transition in a certain measure in a piece of music is from A to E-flat, we can see what it is in the score and check on the tuning fork. But there are no mechanical ways of verifying that the color is cool, that the passage in the music is tense and dramatic. We can inspect the syllables of a line of poetry to see that there is an alliterative effect. Or that the food images predominate in a poem. But do the poetic lines lumber along? What is the effect of the speed of movement of a line or its images on our imagination? Only sensitivity, discrimination, training and experience will provide answers. Further, (ii) the two kinds of properties belong to different logical orders. For example, we can say that the line is nervous and sensitive because, having been etched with a fine steel pen, it is long, dark, hard and thin. We can also say that this passage in the sonata is harmonically tense and dynamic because Haydn moves from G flat, to E and so forth. "The opening lines of this poem seem strained, tense and dramatic *because* the poet has yoked together a sensuous image with a concept." In an alternative way we can say that this portion of the painting is dynamically restless *on account* of the nonserial arrangement of the lines, planes and volumes. We use words like "because" and "on account of." Aesthetic properties thus are seen to be based on nonaesthetic ones.

But this is not wholly the case, for aesthetic properties are not con-dition-governed. The same color may be warm or cold, depending on its contexts. And the same line, in a different context may not have the same character. Moreover, the relationship between the two sorts of properties in each particular case may be clear. In this case the effect *is* restlessness. And it *is* true that the lines convolve cyclically, the planes recede diagonally and that the volumes are distributed precariously and unevenly. Colors set next to each other in one case may be harmonious and in another case be in tension. D. F. Tovey says, "Haydn, like Nature and all great artists, has causes for his effects."[15] And noticing the open-ing shock of a chord and the "strange sense of security" that it passes into, you may find the ingredients which account for it on further investigation. Because we use words like "because" and "on account of," we think we have found that which is re-sponsible for the effect or the factors that make the passage after the initial chord so soothing. But strictly speaking, there are no *causes* (in the mechanical sense) here. Causes are repeatable in other contexts. But aesthetic effects are not invariably repeat-able and they do not come about mechanically. It is true that the aesthetic property and the nonaesthetic properties to which it is related are co-present. But the relationship cannot be envisioned molecularly — as if the atomic particles of nonaesthetic properties by a sheer cumulative arrangement engenders the aesthetic effect. If we envision the relationship in this way, we begin to think of it as universal and repeatable. But to do so is a mistake. (This is one of the ways in which an imitation of an artist or a style can go wrong. The means are captured, but the effect will fall short because the results are not invariable.) Particulars are involved in works of art. And so are unique properties and unique objects. In relating aesthetic to nonaesthetic properties, we come to see the aesthetic properties more clearly, but we cannot form rules. Yet they interest us because they are a part of the appear-ance a thing has.

9) Where there is a subject matter (as in representational works), we are accustomed to mention and describe the objects, events and the attitudes represented. "This is a portrait of the Bishop of Toledo." "When the curtain rises, 'Prince Ivan, on a hunting expedition wanders into an enchanted wood and captures a Firebird. On her pleading, he frees her.'"[16] "Saint, horse, dragon, princes are all in profile."[17] "In the poem, Donne speaks in the persona of a brilliant rake."

10)   The critic, instead of simply mentioning what he wants his listener to see, can resort to colorful speech and flamboyant prose, where there is no clear line between the literal and the figurative.   In point of fact, the language of criticism is fraught with metaphors and quasi metaphors, especially in the delineation of the moods and emotionality of a work of art.   There is nothing illegitimate in the use of metaphors, for, after all, there is no reason why we cannot say that metaphors also "describe," though not literally.   Moreover, figurative speech may be judged to be either appropriate and effective or not.   It is within the control of reason.   By using metaphors, we can make our point more readily, and they are picturesque; they serve the useful function of keeping the prose lively, Agitated violins, frenzied colors and slashes of brushstrokes.   "When the brass bands in the *Tuba Mirum* 'burst out into their antiphonal blazing coruscations, . . . it was as though a thousand rockets had gone up over our heads and were bursting into flames.' "[18]

> On the upbeat, a fanfare begins, like cars a block away honking; the sound drops lower, changed into a pulse. Against it, and against a squiggle like a bit of wallpaper, you hear — as if by free association — a snatch of "Chinatown, My Chinatown", misremembered, on an electric mandolin.   The music sounds confident.   Meanwhile the boys' steps have been exploding like pistol shots.   The steps seem to come in tough, brief bursts. . . . But already two — no, eight — girls have replaced them. Rapidly, they test toe-power, stops on oblique lines, jet-like extensions.   They hang in their air like a swarm of girl-size bees, while the music darts and eddies beneath them.[19]

11)   At the same time, if the occasion demands it, the critic can bring out and make explicit the symbols and allegory in the work.   "To express grief, Bach employs . . . a chromatic progression of five or six notes, typifying torturing grief, and a uniform sequence of notes in pairs, that is like a series of sighs."[20] "The dust pile is a symbol for *Our Mutual Friend*. It dominates even the landscape of London, which has already been presented by Dickens under such a variety of aspects."[21]   Iconological comments in the studies of medieval and Renaissance paintings are further examples.

12)   The symbols mentioned in the preceding paragraph are found within the work of art. But the work of art as a whole can have a meaning and significance which the critic can dutifully discuss at length.   This aspect of criticism is best treated in connection with the idea of interpretation.

We have already said enough to show the taxonomic complexity of analyses and to demonstrate that an object, including a work of art, can be sliced in a number of different ways to accommodate our analytical needs. One further feature of criticism, however, needs to be pointed out. When an analysis seems to get out of hand and become a bit fanciful, or when we do not agree with the critic in his reading of what is under observation, we often say that he has given us an interpretation. In doing so, what we are saying is that he has not given us an analysis or a plain description. Yet analysis and description, synthesis and interpretation are not correlative notions. An elucidation of this statement and a theory of interpretation will occupy us for the rest of this chapter.

II

In analyzing a work of art, we identify the work, its creator, we name the features, mention the parts, point out various facts of the work of art — all of these things by verbal emphasis as well as by gestures. To name the entity, to state the facts, to say what sort of thing it is, to mention what is worth noticing — these are all important aspects of analysis. But they do not describe the work of art. Pointing is not describing, nor is naming. When we describe, "we set forth in words by reference to characteristics";[22] and we give a detailed or graphic account of something. Thus, some of the things we do when we analyze have little or no connection with description. And yet it also appears that when we describe a work of art, we are not always making an analysis. Here is a description by Ruskin of Turner's painting "The Slave Ship."

It is a sunset on the Atlantic, after prolonged storm; but the storm is partially lulled, and the torn and streaming rainclouds are moving in scarlet lines to lose themselves in the hollow of the night. The whole surface of the sea included in the picture is divided into two ridges of enormous swell, not high nor local, but a low broad heaving of the whole ocean, like the lifting of its bosom by deep-drawn breath after the torture of the storm. Between these two ridges the fire of the sunset falls along the trough of the sea, dyeing it with an awful but glorious light, the intense and lurid splendour which burns like gold, and bathes like blood. Along this fiery path and valley, the tossing waves by which the swell of the sea is restlessly divided, lift themselves in dark, indefinite, fantastic forms, each casting a faint and ghastly shadow behind it along the illumined foam. They do not rise everywhere, but three or four together in wild groups, fitfully and furiously, as the under strength of the swell compels or permits them; leaving between them treacherous spaces of level and whirling water, now lighted with green and lamp-like fire, now flashing back the gold of the declining sun, now fearfully dyed from above with the undistinguishable images of the burning clouds, which fall upon them in flakes of crimson and scarlet, and gives to the reckless waves the added motion of their own fiery flying. Purple and blue, the lurid shadows of the hollow breakers are cast upon the mist of the night, which gathers cold and low, advancing like the shadow of death upon the guilty ship as it labours amidst the lightning of the sea, its thin masts written upon the sky in lines of blood, girded with condemnation in that fearful hue which signs the sky with horror, and mixes its flaming flood with the sunlight, and, cast far along the desolate heave of the sepulchral waves, incarnadines the multitudinous sea.[23]

Of this passage, Herbert Read, who is by no means unsympathetic with either Ruskin or Turner, nevertheless was compelled to say that the "wonderful purple patches in description" were a "parallel work of art rather than an analysis, a synthetic vision in which every detail focusses to wonderful clarity."[24] It is true that if we were standing before the painting, Ruskin's outpouring would have reference to the painting, and we would certainly recognize the painting as the one Ruskin is describing. Nevertheless, his emphasis is on the fused, organic view of the work. In being a synthesized view, it tends to become autonomous and to take on an interest of its own. (This is one of the ways in which a synthetic vision resembles an interpretation.)

What is a description? It may be contrasted with a number of different activities:

> Describing vs. evaluating
> Describing vs. emoting
> Describing vs. interpreting
> Describing vs. explaining
> Describing vs. conjecturing
> Describing vs. stating, reporting, asserting, mentioning
> Describing vs. identifying, naming

Since description can be contrasted with many activities that are not identical, it is relatively complex. In order to make clear what description can be, I shall first discuss it in contrast with interpretation — describing and interpreting being the key activities involved in the nonevaluative aspects of art criticism — and leave the first two contrasts above for detailed discussion in later chapters.

First some linguistic evidence will be presented in order to have it before us as the discussion continues. (A) There are things that we can both interpret and describe. (i) We can describe a person's action as well as interpret it. (ii) We can describe an event as well as interpret it. (iii) We can describe a statistical table as well as interpret it.

B) There are things that we can describe but cannot interpret. (i) Many objects: The table at which Jane Austen wrote *Pride and Prejudice*. A pair of shoes. (Contrast with Van Gogh's painting of an old pair of shoes). A maple tree. Time (Contrast with Augustine's theory of time). The state of Oregon. A view from a mountain top. (Contrast with Petrarch's account of his trip to the mountain top as well as what we would say of it.) (ii) Activities: How to roast a duck in the Cantonese manner. How to do the *gigue*. (Contrast with the *gigue* itself as an expression of a certain historical period.) (iii) Persons: Charlotte Corday (as against her life and times). St. Thomas Aquinas (as against his philosophy).

For any of the items in (B), it seems absurd, or nearly so, to ask for an interpretation. One can describe a maple tree in many different ways, depending on the contexts — as a landmark, as a task in botany, etc. But what would it be like to ask sensibly for an interpretation of a maple tree? Or Charlotte Corday? It is not easy to imagine an ordinary context for such requests. Any situation in which one might want an interpretation of a maple tree would be bizarre — say a charade, or a fairy tale pantomime in which kings and gnomes, rhinosceroses and animated maple trees all speak and lead a passional existence. The need for a description of Charlotte Corday takes a different context from an interpretation. A writer in a novel or an actress in a play may present an interpretation of Charlotte Corday. A Marxist writer or a biographer influenced by Freudien psychology might write a biography interpreting the life and character of Charlotte Corday. The interpretation of someone by an actress (a reenactment) is *not* what we usually mean by an interpretation as it occurs in art criticism, though we may compare Gielgud's interpretation of Hamlet with Olivier's. (There is a point of resemblence and a junction between the two senses of interpretation to which we return later on.) Thus, it would initially appear that in describing and in interpreting, two different things are dealt with; and if they should happen to be the same thing, in which case it is viewed from different aspects.

The first question to ask in clarifying the difference is to ask under what sorts of circumstances do the requests for either arise? What are the situations in which a description is needed? Primarily in cases where we have never seen something or done something; for if we know how something looks (or how to do something) there is no need to ask for description. A police officer may say to the victim of a robbery, "Describe your assailant." Or a prospective guest may say, over the phone, "All right, I'll be there at six o'clock but describe the corner where I turn so I'll not get lost." The description given, then should indicate just those features that are salient so that the person or the place would be recognizable. Hearing a description of something we are already familiar with is apt to be boring unless we are for some special reason very fond of the description (as children like to listen to familiar accounts over and over again) or particularly interested in the narrator's reaction. In the case of criticism, particularly when the analysis is performed in the presence of the object, the presumption is, usually, that the listener finds the analysis (and if it partly consists of descriptions, then the description too) helpful in seeing and understanding the object: and the description given analogously serves the function of a picture or a diagram in a technical treatise. Thus in describing, we would not mention everything, but only those features that are relevant to the comprehension of the work of art. Diagrams are drawn to point out the relevant features involved in the discussion, and they differ from case to case, depending on the uses to which it will be put; and so also with descriptions.

What are the situations in which a request for an interpretation arises? "What is behind Senator X's erratic behavior? Do you have an interpretation?" The respondant might have an idea about the Senator's hidden tactics. A news commentator, after describing the Senator's activities, might go on to interpret them. The Pharaoh asked Joseph for an interpretation of his dream. A candidate for confirmation might ask the priest for an interpretation of a doctrine which he found difficult to accept (or understand) in the catechism. The need for an interpretation then arises when something which is already known in some respects is puzzling or does not meet prior expectations. The request then, is for an explanation.

Consider the methods of interpretation used by psychoanalysts. The patient, lying on a couch, narrates a dream. The doctor (as well as the patient) can describe it, but a psychoanalyst is not merely interested in that. The elements of the event (if not the event itself) is taken to be symbolic, and he busies himself in arriving at an interpretation. In describing the dream, the dreamer says: "First there was a horrid man with a dark, stringy beard, holding over me a bloody crucifix. Then the man began to beat me with the crucifix, though I didn't understand the cause of his fury. I made the slightest gesture of resistence, the crucifix broke . . . then I woke up." The dream has been told. A behaviorist would demand that the event be described in terms of recorded electrical activity in the brain, measurable muscular tensions, etc. To a psychiatrist, however, all of these would be both uninteresting and irrelevant. The dream requires an interpretation. A description of the dream is presupposed (i.e. we have a narrative of it); only it is opaque to our understanding and we want a further reading. A Latin poet noted this of dreams by saying

> Dreams, dreams that mock us with their flitting shadows,
> They come not from the temples of the gods. . . .
> Each man makes his own dreams. The body lies
> Quiet in sleep, what time the mind set free
> Follows in darkness what it sought by day.[25]

Freud in his manner said: "When the work of interpretation has been completed the dream can be recognized as a wish-fulfillment." To interpret a dream is to specify its "meaning." His method was to treat a dream as a symptom,[26] where the content of the dream is the fulfillment of a wish. In his interpretation, a psychoanalyst suggests the entities to which the elements of the dream refer. The references are events and thoughts in the life of the persons who had the dream, but the method of interpretation is extrinsic to the dream itself.

A brief list will show that even in interpretations, the elucidation of meaning can proceed in a number of different ways.

a) In interpreting a statistical table, we deduce implications following many mathematical principles, the rules of probability, and facts known about the things tabulated.

b) When we interpret a weather map, we read what the map reports about present air pressures, wind directions, etc., and make predictions about the weather, relying on meteorological theories. The map reports the past and the present but what we deduce is about the future.

c) When I interpret a dream, I spell out its meaning. I interpret the symbols on the basis of what is known about dreams that people in a certain culture seem to have, what is known about their past experiences, and if the context is a therapeutic one, I make a prognosis for a cure.

d) When I interpret a foreign language or a code, I use a dictionary, a grammar, a cipher, etc. Two sets of languages are involved, and I refer from one to the other.

Since it seems plausible to say that an interpretation consists in the elucidations of meanings, it is worthwhile to assess the adequacy of this account.

1) Things that normally cannot be said to have a meaning cannot be interpreted in the ordinary way. This partly accounts for the things that may be described but not interpreted; for tables, the moon, persons, etc., do not have meanings. (In a theatrical sense, we might interpret a maple tree — in the manner of Stanislavsky — or Charlotte Corday as a character in a play. If a biographer has given a new interpretation of the life of Charlotte Corday, or an astrologer an interpretation of the astral events, what they serve up is a new piecing together of the evidence with an overlay of new meanings.)

2) Suppose we were describing some dark thunder clouds. We could say: they are dark and low-hanging; they emit lightening and thunder and are accompanied by cold winds. One might also add: they mean rain, and intend the additional statement to be a part of the description. But we may also say that this is an interpretation. The dark thunder clouds are natural signs with which we are most familiar, and in describing, one could talk about their "meaning."

3) Of verbal utterances, [27] it is difficult to differentiate descriptions from interpretations in the manner suggested because words and utterances by their nature have meanings. The fact of the matter is that only rarely do we ask for the description of verbal utterances. We ask for interpretations: and then only when there is a puzzle or a difficulty of some sort. Unless an unfamiliar word is used, the utterance and its context should be self-explanatory. A slip of the tongue is a case in point. We may describe the situation in which such a social mishap occurred. (This includes a description of what was said — a report). What is uttered is unsuited to the occasion. To say

that it was a slip of the tongue is to offer an interpretation of the event, especially if the slip of the tongue was innocent enough; but the analyst points out ways in which it might reveal (betray) an undesirable hidden thought.

4) If the question concerns the *meaning* of an event or a word, one would be asked to give (indicate) the meaning (which is not to describe it). So this seems to confirm the distinction formulated. Yet, in the final analysis, there is no *one* way in which description and interpretation differ. We have seen that the contexts in which requests for descriptions and interpretations arise differ. But descriptions could be literal or figurative. And both descriptions and interpretations could be used to teach, direct, etc.

5) But there is a totally different function of the notion of interpretation in art criticism. Interpretation plays an argument-stopping role here. Then, to say that an account is an interpretation, *ipso facto,* implies that it is a reading which is not generally made, that it is (even if it is presented impersonally), one which is not related to any facts or any objective data;[28] therefore, it is the expression of a personal opinion. In consequence, any further discussion must be blocked off. What this suggests is that descriptions are more neutral than interpretations. An interpretation is compromised because it involves meanings which in any case require a frame of reference. The extreme case of interpretation (the one concerned here) involves a frame of reference which is incorrigible and is thus purely subjective. A critic described a painting by Picasso in an exhibit in the following way:

> Despite the date on the stretcher, this picture may have been painted early in June 1940. It seems probable from the evidence of drawings made on 4 and 8 June . . . that it reflects Picasso's dismay and anger at the arrival of German troops on the Atlantic coast where he was staying. The extraordinary power in the anatomical inventions and their monumental solidity is increased by the restrained but sinister colouring. The narrow insolent look in the eyes, the distended belly, the aggressive swing of the breasts suggesting the form of a swastika and the horror of the squat legs finishing in enormous ill-formed feet makes this terrifying female a most disquieting image associated with catastrophic events.[29]

In discussing this passage, another critic wrote "Because Picasso did what he had to do and did it with unparalleled virtuosity and fury does not mean that one has to like or even admire all his manifestations, or, having read Roland Penrose's excellent preface to the show, to go along with interpretations such as this one."[30] Surely a like qualm could be raised by the following comments in a program note for a concert:

> The "Music for a mourning spirit" was written with many interruptions during the first years of World War II. The form of the composition is a rather freely handled sonata form. . . . A full analysis is impossible in the available space. Suffice it to say that the title means no more than an indication of the emotional domain with which this music is associated. If one connects the indications, "expectation and lyricism" with "spirit" in the broadest sense of the word, and "oppressive, imperative tone" with Teutonic fascism and its criminality, then the domain of inspiratory impulses is satisfactorily defined. [31]

This road-blocking notion of "interpretation" will be the subject of the following section.

III

"Well, that is his interpretation of the matter."

We say this often, and we imply that we need not accept the explanation. Everything that we experience is wound up in our viewpoint, and viewpoints being personal, such interpretations are not interpersonally binding. In this way, interpretations are incorrigible.

There are a number of reasons why this view of interpretation is plausible and thus prevalent. (We must even grant that it is one strand in ordinary usage.) (i) Events and works of art are often complex and they require elucidations. (ii) And the interpreter, in order to supply these elucidations, must have experience and expertise. (iii) At the same time, most interpretations require a context: the application of an explanatory schema, a cipher, a key, etc. Wherever there are such schemes of explanations, there are bound to be alternative schemes that are applicable, among which a decision is personal. Any or all of these three factors account for the multiplicity of interpretations and the difficulty of deciding among them.

1) But interpretations are corrigible. To begin with, the meanings and elucidations that may be imposed on utterances, events and works of art cannot be purely personal. Whatever interpretations are, if such interpretations are the formulations of meaning, then they must be understandable and rendered inter-

personal. When a meaning put forward is eccentric, we can say, naturally, that the interpreter *thinks* that, because, of course, he does. But we have the right to reject such interpretations. We may say that it is strained and it does not ring true. It isn't plausible at all. In rejecting any interpretation, we must explain ourselves, of course: we are committed to that much, and we cannot merely say that we reject it. Meanings are, after all, communal properties. If an interpretation fits and it enriches our experience and our understanding, we should accept it. We may also accept an interpretation in part only, or simply entertain it — mulling over it because we have not seen exactly how it works yet. But eventually, if we decide, it is because we see it to be plausible or implausible.

2) Strictly speaking, events as well as works of art, may be taken in any way one wishes. But not all ways are equally significant or sensible. We may use works of art subjectively as we use Rorschach tests. But an event seen historically, an action seen pragmatically, or an art object taken aesthetically are not such subjective modes. Historical and political interpretations are guided by the principles of historical and political studies, and they are not occasions for subjective outpourings, though, to be sure, a historian has his political and moral commitments as a person. A work of art too is not merely a subjective entity — something that can be a work of art for one person and for no one else in the world. If this were the case, then in order to understand an interpretation, we would have to look at the psychology of the interpreter. If art criticism is wholly a matter of interpretation, then we must look at the art critic, not the work of art, to understand critical discourse. All criticism, if this were so, would consist of psychological autobiographies of the critics.[32] Notice that we examine the personal beliefs of a critic only where an interpretation seems to have gone drastically wrong. This presupposes that some interpretations can be *seen* definitely to be wrong and others to be relatively correct.

3) Interpretations cannot merely be the reporting of psychological states, whether it be the critic's, the artist's or any other person's. Notice that we correct misinterpretations, even in an imaginative reading, by referring to the work of art, and this rechecking seems to be a matter of closer scrutiny. Even if the process is "imaginative insight," when we imaginatively look, we simply look more alertly. We are not trying to see what no one else sees. If a critic were to *imagine* anything *not* in the work of

art (an imagination gone wild), we would call that judgment invalid and begin to distrust his critical acumen. Even when we hallucinate, the fact of hallucination is something that we can discover. Seeing the art object imaginatively is no different in kind from seeing it any other way, except in richness of association.

In line with this thought, some critical theorists have looked upon aesthetic interpretations as the re-creation of the imaginative process of the artist — that is, we must imaginatively put ourselves in the place of the artist, reconstructing his psychological state in the act of creation. But it is clear that we do not need actually to undergo the mental states suffered by VanGogh, Bosch, Franz Kafka or Dostoievsky to appreciate their landscapes or their internal visions. Neither is such a repetition necessary to understand them adequately or to decide whether or not an interpretation is accurate. (And can we literally reconstruct the creative processes of a Dante, a Michaelangelo or a Shakespeare?) There are also cases in which an artist meant the work of art to be one thing, and we see it not to be so at all — Milton's view of God, perhaps, or Huckleberry Finn as an expression of pure childhood innocence. In such cases, there is no *necessary* congruence between the work of art and the imaginative process of the artist. There would be such a congruence between the psychological process of the poet and the so-called "content" of the poem, for example, if the poem were a pure lyrical expression of the poet's experience.

> And my lament
> Is cries countless, cries like dead letters sent
> To dearest him that lives alas! away.
>
> I am gall, I am heartburn. God's most deep degree
> Bitter would have me taste: my taste was me;
> Bones built in me, flesh filled, blood brimmed the curse.[33]

Then, even the description of the lexicographical meanings of the poem would resemble the psychological process of the poet in the act of creation. (The case would be neater still if the poem, and such there are, were a poem about the writing of a poem.) In such cases, reading the poem would be interpreting it, just as acting out Lear is interpreting the play *King Lear*. But these examples would be appropriate only if the poet in writing a poem were merely experiencing the emotions he is writing about, and in the "white heat" of creation there is a minimum of objectified calculation of effects — of how to put the words, the accents and rhymes together. Poems that are purely expressive and evocative in this manner are rare, and even in those cases one should still wish to distinguish the poem from the poet and his act of creation from the response of the reader, though they would all tend, perhaps, to resemble each other.

4) Many interpretations require the introduction of an external scheme, as in the reading of a foreign language or in the deciphering of a code. But not all interpretations are, in this manner, exterior. It is true that if an unfortunate slip of the tongue is claimed by a Freudian analyst to have libidinal references, we can reject this interpretation on the grounds that we do not accept the Freudian account of motivation. If all interpretations require some external reference, then it might be possible *in principle* always to reject any interpretation as questionable. Perhaps all interpretations are constructions, and there are always alternative constructions possible, including the most fanciful ones.

In most interpretations, however, our primary interest lies on the entity itself. We try to exercise our intelligence and ingenuity in order to explain or draw inferences from a fabric of signs, a set of numbers in a table, a series of casual events. Our intelligence includes our ability to utilize our past experiences fully. But in interpreting a statistical table, we do not need to concern ourselves with the mental states of the writer. We need only examine the sets of numbers, their interrelationships, and we deduce the meaning of the table. We pay attention only to the statistical table. If statistical interpretation is suspect because our knowledge of the laws of probability and our entire past experience (all of which are external) are necessary to it, then any act of intelligence is made suspect. In all of these cases, we should, instead, be willing to say that the truth involved is intrinsic.

Particularly with works of art, interpretations do not always require an external reference. The meaning must be contained in the work of art. So any reading of it must be supported by the work of art itself. The kinds of meaning that may be generated differ greatly depending on the media utilized. But if works of art are by their nature autonomous, it must be possible to spell out their meaning from within. For example, in interpreting a poem, we discuss the world contained in it, especially the system of emotional stresses created by it. Suppose we are interpreting the following poem.

The Windhover:
To Christ Our Lord

I caught this morning morning's minion, king-
    dom of daylight's dauphin, dapple-dawn-drawn Falcon, in his
    riding
Of the rolling level underneath him steady air, and striding
High there, how he rung upon the rein of a wimpling wing
In his ecstacy! then off, off forth on swing,
    As a skate's heel sweeps smooth on a bow-bend: the hurl and
    gliding
    Rebuffed the big wind. My heart in hiding
Stirred for a bird, — the achieve of, the mastery of the thing!

Brute beauty and valour and act, oh, air, pride, plume, here
    Buckle! AND the fire that breaks from thee then, a billion
Times told lovelier, more dangerous, O my chevalier!

    No wonder of it: shéer plód makes plough down sillion
Shine, and blue-bleak embers, ah my dear,
    Fall, gall themselves, and gash gold-vermilion.³⁴

We might say of this poem; the Falcon in our poem is Christ
who is also the lovely chevalier. As a result of buckling (breaking)
in the crucifiction, he breaks into the splendid fire of his resur-
rection. If there is a question about this reading, how do we
decide? We can say: The Falcon is, of course, only a bird that
the poet saw flying in the dawn, whose ease and charm in the
air reminded him of a cavalier. The poem is dedicated to Christ
Our Lord. But that only shows that the poet was religious and
that he thought the poem good enough to be a gift for Christ.
Honneger dedicated his oratorio *Jeanne d'Arc au bûcher* to the
dancer Madame Ida Rubinstein, but that in no way means that
Joan is really Madame Rubinstein. The falcon is simply the
falcon and nothing else. And the fire is certainly not the splendor
of a risen God or any such thing. To say otherwise is to read
into the poem. Any decision we might reach, even to withhold
judgment, must be guided by the poem itself. We notice, for
example, that the word "Falcon" is capitalized, but the word
"chevalier" is not. Why is there a colon between the words "The
Windhover" and "To Christ our Lord"? Is the interpretation
farfetched? We look at the poem to see which view gives us the
richest, most coherent and most plausible account. The meaning
is internal to the poem, and the interpretation must arise from it.
    5) Another sort of claim has been made about interpretation:
that all criticism, at least in part if not wholly, is a matter of

interpretation. The view has been supported in two ways. (A) In art criticism, the object of art is before us and to describe it is useless. What we require is an interpretation. "Interpreting is not describing; this is unnecessary, the critic assumes a direct acquaintance, past or possible, with the work he interprets. Therefore, the critic's problem is to draw attention, not describe."[35] But I have already shown (in section I of this chapter) that in an analysis of a work of art, the work is described and that a description is often helpful. (B) But a more crucial reason is that there can never be a work of art "apart from *some* interpretation." This assertion combines two considerations: that "the work of art is what it is interpreted to be," though not all interpretations count; and that any "interpretation is partly subjective invention."[36] These considerations are bolstered by a number of observations:

(i) Works of art are esoteric things; and interpretations and evaluations of them are never complete. Therefore each age, each generation, needs to interpret the art of the past and its tradition anew. Further, (ii) each culture, each society, must interpret the art of another for itself. Our view of Chinese art is not that of the Chinese themselves. What is important about a work of art — our viewing of a Renoir, our reading of a sonnet by Shakespeare — is our experience of it; in short, our interpretation of it. Interpretative criticism must therefore be a creative, constructive rather than an objective act. Furthermore, (iii) if works of art are unique, so must our experiences of them be unique and different. We notice also that, ontologically, many of the non-plastic arts require an interpretation (though this is granted to be the introduction of a different, though related sense of interpretation) for their actual momentary existence: this feature constitutes part of the very nature of these works of art. It is what make them individually unique. A piece of music needs to be played (interpreted) in order to come into being, and each performance will have subtle differences.[37] The work of art requires this creation; and this is also true of all criticism. "To judge a work of art, therefore, is to give a verdict on something to which the judge has contributed and this also 'justifies' the verdict."[38] Each interpretation is individual. There is no such thing as the *real* work of art.[39]

A number of comments need to be made here. (i) The sense in which a musical composition and play are interpreted is different from the sense in which a critic interprets a work of art. Music in order to exist requires an interpretation. The musician

presents or displays the music by performance.   He gives a
reading. It may be said the critic does so too, since in interpreting a
poem or a novel, he "presents" it or "displays" it.   But the
terms relate only analogously. The critic's reading is an explanation, it is referential: it is not *the* work of art itself as is the
case with the particular realization of a play or a musical piece.
(ii) It is true that in the performing arts, works must be
performed in order for them to come into being; and since
each performance is an individual event, all performances arc
unique.   But performances themselves can be, and must be,
evaluated on the basis of their faithfulness to the spirit as well
as the letter of the score or the text and in terms of the expressive
coherence and effectiveness of the actual performance. Therefore,
even works that are said to be unique can be adjudicated and
evaluated.   Their interpretation is not sheer chaos, nor is it incorrigible subjectivism.

   iii)   What is more, in the sense that criticism contains an
interpretation, not all works of art can be interpreted. What would
it be like to interpret the *Venus de Milo,* a skyscraper, a Sung
Dynasty vase (except fancifully or in the context of a historical
or sociological exposition)?   Even a Renoir, a Siennese painting
(a Sasseta) defy interpretation. One may describe them evocative-
ly.   One may show forth their form, their dewy freshness.   But
it is hard to say that these things have "meanings" and to that
extent, it is awkward to speak of interpretation.   If we were to
interpret them, we would probably be writing an account of them
not as works of art but as incidents in the life of Renoir or
phases in the history of painting in Tuscany, etc.   Confronted
by these works, one wants simply to look.   And if one cannot
see them, then he wants to be made to see them.

   iv)   At this point, we begin to realize the importance of
explication and minute analysis of a work of art.   In a fine and
detailed explication (like those presented by D. F. Tovey) the
process is most like an elaborate fabric weaving (construction)
showing a complex interrelationship among the parts.   A critical
essay without any particular examples cannot be very helpful.
To a great extent, the more particularized and the more concrete
the art criticism, the more satisfactory it is.   This is why detailed
explication in poetry or formal analysis in music is so helpful.
Such an activity places the premium on the "understanding" of
the work of art and we are made to see all that there is to be
seen.   There are criticisms, of course, which deal with the complete

46

works of a man or even the art of an epoch. Such discussions, however, are helpful only to persons who have studied the works of the man or the art of a whole period in detail. These discussions are apt to be, for the most part, unsatisfactory, unless considerable details and illustrations are furnished.

v) I suspect that some philosophers insist that criticism must be called interpretation because the critic evaluates when he points out. And if he indicates a judgment, he cannot be describing.[40] A critic says:

> Nor, the pattern once assured, has Giotto failed of vivid dramatic presentation. It is surprising to find crowded into so small a space so many new poses all beautifully expressive of the individual shades of a common feeling: the woman to the left of the cross leaning her head on her hand as though sorrow had become a physical pain; the beautiful figure of the youth, with long waving hair, who throws back both arms with a despairing gesture; the woman lifting her robe to wipe her tears; and, most exquisite of all, the most surprising, in its novelty and truth to life, the figure of the girl to the left, drawn towards the terrible scene by a motion of sympathy and yet shrinking back with instinctive shyness and terror.[41]

To call this describing, it might be thought, would be misleading because the passage cumulatively implies a judgment. By drawing our attention to various features, asking us to see certain relations and, of course, suggesting that these things are worth attending to (for they intensify *our* experience), the critic is commending. After all, we do not usually point at things not worth noticing. This is true even of the adverse critical remark that Fry goes on to make: "In the child alone Giotto has, as was usually the case, failed of a rhythmical and expressive pose." Whether the tone of the passage is commendatory or not, Fry either speaks appropriately and accurately or he does not. And in order to decide this question we must look at the painting. Fry points out the various interesting features of the painting, and that constitutes description.

IV

We usually describe a work of art for a listener who is less experienced than we are or for a reader who cannot have the work before him. But when we state that this is by Mozart, it was written in 1780, this is a sonnet, this is the head of Holofernes, we are not describing. We are simply saying what something is and naming objects, with an appropriate pointing. But we describe, too. We bring to the notice of the viewers features to which he might not have attended or might not have known how to attend, and we do this by verbally going over the object — so that he will soon notice too. Normally we would not describe obvious things, though, for example, in the analysis of a novel (because its length makes a concerted attention of the whole difficult) the course of events, the characters of the principals have to be described often.

The identity that most people (critics as well as ordinary lovers of art) make between interpretations and syntheses is a natural one. In a synthetic view, one gives an account of the work that is unified, overarching and harmonious. One discusses the object as a whole and often in relation to other works of the creator or other works of the times. In an interpretation, the critic delineates the meaning of the work of art, in part and in whole. And in spinning out its meaning, he takes note of the parts in their context; he views the relation of the parts so that they should influence and bear on each other. Any account short of one that takes in the whole work of art will only be a tentative reading. The critic should weave together a fabric of meaning— a tapestry which presents a whole picture. Thus synthesis and interpretation are alike in having an eye toward the whole work of art.

But in the final analysis, the discourse of an ideal critic should have a seamless unity and harmony. We believe that the staple of criticism lies in analysis. Such analysis may in its larger design emphasize the impressions and responses of the critic, the contexts in which the work of art might reasonably be placed; or in its detail, may consist of an objective, formal description and anatomization of the object. At the same time, in describing, the critic "would set forth in words by reference to various characteristics present," an intenser awareness of the work of art. In so doing, he analyzes, but he could as well give an account which is more holistic (a synthesis). The term description covers both activities, as is made evident in the example from Ruskin (section II of this chapter); and I see no need to withdraw this term from what such a critic does. From this summary, it is clear that the contrasts usually drawn between analysis and synthesis, and description and interpretation cannot be maintained sharply.

They cut across each other at several points: for in an analysis we may describe as well as interpret. But in describing, we may analyze as well as synthesize. In point of fact, interpretation and description, analysis and synthesis all go hand in hand.

4 | SUBJECTIVE ELEMENTS

Wallace Stevens says in his poem "Peter Quince at the Clavier"

> Just as my fingers on these keys
> Make music, so the selfsame sounds
> On my spirit make a music, too.
>
> Music is feeling, then, not sound;
> And thus it is that what I feel,
> Here in this room, desiring you,
>
> Thinking of your blue-shadowed silk,
> Is music . . .[1]

Peter Quince's meditation seems very special. But if music is feeling reverberating in one's spirit, not the sound one hears, then the most essential portion of music is an internal event, a personal response which must be felt. This thesis is familiar: that music as art is what moves us. There is another striking example from *Madame Bovary*. Emma was completely absorbed in the performance of *Lucia di Lammermoor;* letting herself "be lulled by the melodies, feeling herself vibrate to the very fiber of her being, as though the bows of the violins were playing on her nerve-strings."[2] At the climax of the scene with the sextet, she "herself uttered a sharp cry that was drowned in the blast of the final chords"; and the plight of Lucia evoked memories of her own flighty marriage and she thought

> If only in the freshness of her beauty, before defiling herself in marriage, before the disillusionment of adultery, she could have found some great and noble heart to be her life's foundation! . . . But that kind of happiness was doubtless a lie, invented to make one despair of any love. Now she well knew the true paltriness of the passions that art painted so large. So she did her best to think of the opera in a different light.[3]

But, of course, to no avail, for she was Emma Bovary, capable only of a self-indulgent response to both life and art.

The samples can be extended to all of the other arts. In each case there is an emphasis on our emotional responses; and seeing this, many aestheticians (and laymen too) have concluded that an emotional response characterizes the function of art. It has been described variously. Tolstoy, for one, calls it an emotional infection.[4] But others have called it aesthetic feeling, lyrical expression, empathy, objectified pleasure. In all of these cases, what is emphasized is, on the one hand (at the weakest), the occurrence of an emotional response (or a feeling), and on the other extreme, a fused, overpowering experience of being identified or being carried away by the work of art. In either case, there must be a personal response. And another doctrine goes along with this. We notice that our emotional responses are not all alike, even to the same work. So we conclude further that our responses are personal: and there must be, inevitably, a subjective residue in our experiences of works of art, for feelings and emotions are internal and private.

In this chapter. I examine a number of related notions: what is involved in the idea of a response to a work of art, the respects in which they may be said to be subjective, and the techniques we have for overcoming this subjectivity.

I

It is certainly true that every work of art is responded to by somebody. Works of art to which no one responds would be more than odd. They would be mystifying. As art, they must be available to some path of cognition. We see them and note our seeing of them. We hear them and listen. Or we read them and understand. Standing before a painting, our eyes register the presence of the canvas with a layer of paint spread over it. This physical sense of response is minimal. We also see what there is as a form and representation in the painting. This is a response too. We also respond emotionally. Seeing what there is to be seen and emotionally responding are not easily separated. Yet frequently we are certain that we understand a painting, and it still leaves us unmoved; it does nothing for us. On the contrary there are people who emotionally respond and do not *see* the work of art at all. (They react to the name of the artist, are swayed by the crowd about them, or are triggered by the idea of subject matter attached to the work.) It also happens that in some cases we take in a work of art, see that it is great, and do not feel anything like an emotion. There is room for all of these variations and more.

What we need to do, then, is to carefully set apart the various kinds of responses, since what we call a response covers a complex set.

1) We see, touch, hear and feel objects, all in the perceptual sense. We feel the marble, the rough texture of the welded iron. We hear the sounds of the instruments. We see the rough red pigment. These are sensations. But we also see objects: the painting on a canvas, as well as what is represented there. We hear the melody as well as the counterpoint. These are two logical orders of response: to smell a scent and to smell a rose; to feel the prickly rough surface and to feel rusting iron. Both orders are properly said to be felt and seen and by our bodily sense organs. To some degree, our perceptual language here is poor (though does it *need* to be richer?) and we refer to the sensation by referring to the objects that would give rise to that sensation. It tastes salty, it feels metallic, it makes a grating sound or a shattering noise, it has a velvety look. It is well to keep in mind that even at the lowest point, our perceptual responses already include a number of different levels.

2) We hear: but we also listen. We see: but we also look. We feel: but we also feel for something. Along with the perceptual activities of seeing and touching, and also in contrast with them, there are these "exploratory" uses of sensory terms. There is an intentionality involved in exploratory activities. In ordinary English, it is possible for me to be looking right at something and not notice it. But I could not be looking for something or looking at something and *not* be aware of what I am

52

trying to do. It is possible for me to be hearing a sound (like the ticking of a clock) or seeing something and not notice it because I am engrossed in something else. But it would be logically impossible for anyone to be listening to the sound and *not be aware of doing so.* When I look at a painting, I am more than seeing it. There is a consciousness of the activity involved. I am attending to my seeing, although it may be that I do not know precisely what I may achieve, as is often the case with works of art. When I am looking at something, I am studying it. I look at the *Guernica* to see what there is to be noticed. When I listen to music, I pay attention to what there is to be heard: I listen to the melody, the orchestral coloration, and I look for the harmonic changes.

3) Aestheticians say that we feel the sensuous properties of the work of art, in which, by the sensuous properties (say of a painting), they mean only the various colors and juxtaposition of colors that we see. We could therefore also say that we *feel the sensations;* but this is poor English and it would be less awkward to say that we *have the sensations.* In discussing the sensuous ingredients of music as distinguished from noise, Prall discusses the velocity of the sound waves, the regularities in the frequencies that are discoverable in the sounds that we have selected for the musical scale, and the qualities of the sound waves that account for the timbre of musical sounds. [5] These constitute the physical qualities that separate one sound from another (though these sounds as such may not be aurally distinguishable by our naked ears). We merely hear sounds. But it is obvious on further reflection that we need to distinguish the sensory aspects of the media (that which we refer to by the term "sensation") from the sensuous quality of the media. For some of the art media (particularly literature) presents us with a poverty of sensuous surfaces. There is nothing particularly sensuous about the language of prose, though it is true that as regards our sensory apparatus, there are sensations involved in listening to a work of literature in prose. It is symptomatic of the difference between sensations and sensuous properties that in describing the sensuous properties of a work of literature, we naturally do so by mentioning the images, metaphors and arrangements of meanings and not the physical qualities of the sounds involved; while in the case of painting or music, we need only mention the sensory qualities of the media (we normally do so by pointing

out the instruments of the orchestra, the colors of the pigments, etc.) which by their very nature are already concrete and particular.

As contrasted with sensation, the sensuous involves richness and delight. What music or painting have in more abundance as contrasted with literature (and poetry as contrasted with prose) is a sensuousness of the media — i.e., intrinsic surface richness and delightfulness. In themselves, the sounds of the oboe are luxurious; but not so the sound even of a word like "wealthy." But there is a further complication. Even among colors, not all sensory qualities are equally sensuous. For some painters manage to use black as a color, but others cannot. And in many works of art, the colors are dead; they are not vivid, not sensuous. Some painters, for this reason, are colorists and others are not. Further, the capacity for awareness of sensuousness differs from person to person. In a concert hall, for example, all those present hear sounds though not all listen to the music; and some members of the audience are better aware of the sensuous qualities of the music than others.

4) The responses described above are said to be felt. But the words "feel" and "feeling" are highly equivocal. (A) They may be specific occurrences[6] that are related to bodily sensations. I might feel a thrill on hearing a trumpet voluntary, a tightening of the throat when the heroine dies in a novel, prickling of my skin, chills, goose pimples when the arms of the monster appear in a Frankenstein film. (B) But there is a further sense of feeling that refers to more general conditions, such as feeling sad (on listening to a Mozart adagio), feeling happy, peaceful, joyful, uneasy or bored. These are not associated with any bodily sensations but are rather mood features. (C) A third sense of feeling refers to attitudes, such as approval and disapproval, liking and disliking, enjoying and being repelled. On the emotive theory of value, all forms of valuing, preferring and holding worthwhile are to be included among these. How these differences operate in critical discourse is discussed in section IV.

II

The emotional response that we frequently make to a work of art can be overemphasized. The expression theory of art as developed by both aestheticians and laymen is that the artist is expressing his pent up emotions (that which needs to be released) and that we as connoisseurs must feel the corresponding emotion. Recent movements in the arts — expressionism in painting (including action painting), the theatre of the absurd, *musique concrète* — tend to reinforce this impression. Having formed the conviction, we turn to the history of the various arts and notice all the ways in which the monuments of the past fit our emotionalistic view of art. Many works of art are overwhelming. Who would not be bowled over by the great choral scene in Verdi's *Otello* where Othello abuses Desdemona before the Venetian ambassador and the gathered throng? Many people are stunned by their first view of El Greco's *A View of Toledo* (the colors of the picture are absolutely dazzling, and what shocks us is the unexpected brilliance of the cleaned painting after the dullness of the reproductions to which we have been accustomed). Though these experiences are exciting and valuable, they are not typical of all works of art. Works like Beethoven's *Missa Solemnis* or Mozart's *Don Giovanni* with their touches of the sublime are rare. Quieter and more ordinary are our responses to portraits by Velásquez; landscapes by Claude Lorraine; a cubist design by Picasso; a Mondrian abstraction; a slow piece of music by Mozart; classical Chinese or Greek ceramics. If responses to all of these are to be called emotional responses, then the varieties are indeed very large. We may respond with sensuous delight (Monet); exotic wonderment and enchantment (Gauguin); a surprised amusement (Breughel); wry bemusement (Toulouse-Lautrec, Sharaku); a plain fascination (Calder's ingenuity); a puzzled fascination (Klee). And many responses for which we have no words. On reading Keats' sonnet "To one who has been long in city pent" or on listening to some Bach preludes and fugues (from the *Well-tempered Clavier*) one's response may be that his inner self becomes still, transparent and empty, and any emotion as such is imperceptible. We usually *listen* to a Bach fugue with rapt attention and no more. We of course do respond (i.e. attend); but we do not always respond emotionally, yet our response is no less aesthetic. By virtue of ordinary language, the label "response" can be made to cover all of these varieties. At the same time, we highly value the overwhelming transport that we experience before certain works of art. For one thing, they are especially memorable. Inevitably, then, we think that all responses must be characterized by the memorable sort. But there is no reason to suppose that this is so. Why need we respond to a Bach fugue or the "Casta Diva" from

Norma (Bellini) in the same way that we respond to the "Et resurrexit" from the *B-minor Mass* (Bach) or the climax of *Tristan und Isolde?* The responses obviously need not be identical nor be distinct members of one species.

In many cases (including some which have been cited) our response consists in noticing unperturbed the objects; and we are aware that we are noticing. We see, we listen; we savour our seeing; we appreciate the object and we enjoy it. But none of this constitutes emotions. There are, of course, works of art which when we listen to them or see them give us a shock, a revulsion; but not all of our responses are of that sort. Thus any claim that the essence of a work of art lies in the feeling and emotions we experience must be questionable; for the cases on hand do not support such an assertion.

III

What would be an example of a response that was purely personal? In answering this question we think first of responses that are matters of taste: the way a person responds to some food, the way a person perceives its various properties, or the way he finds them pleasant or unpleasant. We claim that these are purely personal responses because there is great variety in the perceptions of people, their perceptions change over the years, and much of this change is "culture dependent."

It is not clear to what extent the subjectivity of response is due to cultural dependence. If a person's very reaction to a sensation (say turpentine flavored water) is culture-dependent, then we might assume that the response is relatively uniform within a specified group of persons and consequently, that it is no longer merely a personal matter. It is also the case that in matters of food, many of our preferences stem from reasons of health, economy, supply and demand, etc., and are therefore beyond the purely personal.

To find a response that is purely subjective is difficult. Before we go on, it would be worth considering what is implied in saying that a response is *personal,* and that it is *purely personal.* What does the word *purely* add? It amounts to saying that such an experience is privileged in being nonshareable, nonveridical and incorrigible. The following six statements are parts of the claim:

A1)   That no one else need respond in that particular way.

56

A2) The response of another person could have been different; *and* there *are* such different ways. (And by parity of reasoning, the same person, at another time could respond in another way.)

A3) We sometimes discover similarities in responses; but such uniformity of responses have been conditioned and they are learned responses.

B) Personal responses are private.

C1) The response is unveridical and does not need to be justified, defended, explained, etc.

C2) Among alternative responses there is nothing to choose.

The statements above have beeen grouped into three since they are related to each other. And as I spell out their interconnections, the place held by the notion of subjectivity in the grammar of criticism will become apparent.

A) There are many personal, individual responses to works of art. We imply, then, that such responses are not ordinary—that they are subjective and not universal.

1) There are many associations to work of art that are based on private experience. A detail in a painting — the eyes of a man, the flowers in the background, the landscape, the house, the character of a protagonist in a novel — any one of these may recall some memory of a childhood experience and the emotion associated with it. "I don't really have much of a feeling for Robert Frost's 'Birches' and 'On Stopping in the Woods on a Snowy Evening' " a person might say, "because I grew up in the tropics." "I don't really know any Russians and so I can't appreciate Goncharov's *Oblomov.*" A person may dislike Brahms' *Hungarian Dances* because once in a summer resort, he was subjected to them, over and over again, played on a phonograph by an unpleasant person in a neighboring room.

2) The following special responses are also personal associations, but they are worth keeping apart from the above examples. A religious person may respond to certain works of art (which are non-religious) in a religious manner; that is, they have a special interest for him. An Irish Catholic may respond in a special way to a historical novel about medieval life or to novels set in Ireland. A Marxist who sees everything in the light of the dialectic or a Freudian who sees everything psychoanalytically may also have special responses.

3) Independent of any association, one may simply dislike

certain colors or combinations of colors; or he may be particularly fond of certain instrumental tones, say, the whine of bagpipes.

4) There are differences in the degree and the way a person is embarrassed by pictures and statuettes of nudes or graphic sexual passages in a novel. A person may find (many do) the scatological portions of Swift and Rabelais difficult to face. Many people do not like (and thus find it difficult to pay attention to) certain subject matters: generously proportioned, luscious nudes (Rubens, Renoir), paintings of animals or flowers, the monumental, historical paintings of battles, the proletarian novel, or discussions of certain political ideas.

5) Certain art forms make people uncomfortable: the ballet because it seems effeminate; the opera because it is such an "exotic and irrational entertainment"; medieval reliquaries because they are associated with superstition.

Two things need to be noted. Sometimes a "special meaning" is attached to a feature of a work of art. The meaning may be relatively specific. "That seascape reminds me of the summers in my childhood." "That man in the portrait looks like Uncle Sylvester — what a monster he was!" "Little Phoebe in *Catcher in the Rye* reminds me of my little sister." But there are also associations that are more nebulous — auras of nostalgia, twinges of uneasiness, or subliminal lurkings of nameless fears and anxieties.

In saying that these are personal responses, that some of them are idiosyncratic associations, no claim is made of their relevance or irrelevance. Whether they are relevant or not, must be decided independent of their subjectivity. Our response to the scatological passages in Swift and our understanding of the religious and political contexts of the novels of Dostoievsky make a difference in an analysis of these works and are thus relevant to an evalution of the analysis. But most of the special associations listed above cannot be shared by very many persons. To the extent that we can sift out the relevant associations, the quality of individual responses are both inspectable and assessable. It is a fact that we teach others how to respond, we indicate what is worth responding to, and we compare their responses. (The whole process of art education and art criticism presupposes this.) This is not to deny, of course, that, when present, these associations make a difference in our responses and influence them.

To be able to say that certain of our responses and associations are irrelevant implies that some responses are better than others. But the fact that we teach others to respond in certain ways and that we ask people to disregard some of their reactions is evidence that there is an initial element of relativity. This is particularly evident in the necessary re-evaluations made by every generation of the artistic accomplishments and art criticism of the past. For example, the change in taste at the turn of the century was considerable. In evaluating past criticisms of the music of Brahms, a recent critic writes:

> But since 1905 two things have happened against which no author could guard himself: first, our view of the composer and his music has been amplified and sometimes modified as new sources of information became available; secondly, Brahms himself has receded in historical perspective. . . . Inevitably the point of view has changed.[7]

There must then be something arbitrary.

Now is this so? To say that "the way one responds is arbitrary" must be to the say that response might have been otherwise. And in support of this, it is clear that there are many special associations attached to a work of art. That these change is clear also. But it is difficult to ascertain whether in all cases, or even in a great many, alternative, different responses are possible. One might take the case of music. We listen to a cluster of sounds and we seek a pattern. Would *any* pattern do? In a sense the answer is yes: for there are alternative types of musical scales. We can see that different selections of musical intervals and values have made possible the Balinese gamelan, African polyrhythmic music, and Chinese music; tonalism and atonalism; or the deep philosophical approach to music that constitutes the Hindu ragas. The patterns may emphasize different tones, different timbres or rhythms. But can we do *otherwise* than seek patterns of some sort? For this is what is meant by being able to do otherwise: the other arbitrary way. And that this *is* possible is not obvious.

If we think of music as a special kind of aural experience, then the patterns and lines of development possible are limited, for the musical cultures that have been developed are limited in number. There is the western European tradition (which has a number of subtraditions), the Indian-Javanese, the Chinese, the various African patterns and a few more. Certain approaches have been richer, and these have evolved elaborately. But the developments are not merely due to the musical orientation of these cultures; certain patterns in themselves offered richer possibilities of development than others. Fortunately, these alternative patterns are open to anyone who wishes to master them. Note the spread of the comprehension and appreciation of western European orchestral music or of jazz. Music is to a great degree intercultural. But this point hinges on the concept of what music as an art is: as organized entities and as experiences that we structure in certain ways.

B) Personal responses are said to be ultimately private. How can anyone really know what it is that I see and feel when I see a painting by Gauguin? Or how can anyone really know what I hear — that peculiarly woody, mellow, warm sound that I experience — when I listen to an oboe in an accompaniment of an aria by Gluck? I may even go so far as to ask whether even I myself can ever rediscover (or relive) the thrill that I once experienced on reading a novel or the excitement of seeing my first Shakespeare play. The second experience, though it resembles the first, is never exactly like it. So one can never even check up on oneself, let alone on another person.

But what does it mean to say, in the above fashion, that one's responses are nonveridical? If I say that my responses to a new Balanchine ballet was of a certain sort, my saying so should be reason enough for your taking my word for it. About what can one be in doubt? And under what sort of conditions would the doubt arise? I may fail to communicate my responses accurately. Or in order to win an argument, I may be dishonest. But barring these conditions, there should be no doubt. We discover by comparing notes that someone's description of his response is inadequate. Suppose I say that my responses were such an such and you find them not quite like yours; then you will tell me so, and we compare our reactions. In doing so, I might discover that what you say is more accurate (and also fits my experience). This is how one might discover that his ability (perhaps) in describing his reaction is not very good. One discovers this by finding that there are better descriptions. (Journalists often make this discovery. In the haste of writing in order to meet a dateline, they often misreport what they feel. On rereading what they have written, they discover that it does not represent what they intended or that it is misleading, etc.)

If I should say that I liked the new ballet by Balanchine, you have the right to ask me why. Should you do so, I would then try to answer your question I would try to bring out the quality of my experience and the features of the ballet that struck me as interesting, pleasant, puzzling or in other ways worth remarking. What I say, of course, cannot *be* the experience itself, exactly. (In this sense, no two experiences are identical, and it would be absurd to expect them to be.) There is, moreover, a surprisingly rich vocabulary to transmit such information. Sometimes, of course, one has to forge such a vocabulary.

A brief digression about the foregoing of a language: There is a high degree of conventionality in the language of criticism—in the vocabulary for discussing the media, the form, the technique, as well as in the discussion of styles. We have a standard set of terms and adjectives for describing the poetry of the neoclassics or the paintings of the Baroque period. The vocabulary may be unsatisfactory; but the fact of the matter is that there is such a vocabulary, and the neophyte must learn it. When a drastically new style emerges or we evolve a new intention in an art form, the misunderstanding of the public and the confusion of the art lover consist mostly in their inability to talk about the art because of the absence of a vocabulary. The lack of it may impede perception and comprehension of the work of art as well. We know the problems we encounter in talking about any of the arts. To begin with, the language for discussing any of the nonverbal arts is unsatisfactory. We find insurmountable difficulties, even in describing the effect of poetry. Furthermore, we have a body of entities that are novel and bewildering, and, at the beginning of their history, possessed of characteristics that are not easy to enjoy. We do not even know how to look at these works. One's initial reaction is to leave them alone.

This is the state of much criticism at the present time. Leaving aside the questions of whether *musique concrète* and electronic music are "music" or not, they are indeed very much unlike music that we are familiar with. The process of getting used to them involves a number of different things: (i) becoming familiar with the sounds; (ii) learning to see the patterns and intentions involved in the art; (iii) formulating a mode of describing them so that we can begin to discuss these effects. The art of the most recent of the abstractionists and expressionists (of all breeds) has posed such a problem to a number of critics, and many interesting experiments have been performed in aesthetic journalism. A critic can only try.

> Her [Georgia O'keefe] paintings still breathe the pellucid distilled oxygen of a cleared and resonant Southwest, a country that

sometimes comes close to Kafka's "Nature Theatre of Oklahoma," in *Amerika*. . . . *White Patio with Red Door* is O'keefe's Precisionist side, a calm delight in the clear-edged happenstances of her scene. *Two Austrian Copper Roses, 3* is another of her pollinated helicopter-dives onto the portals of flowers, shadowed by the presence of loving observation. But art doesn't have the last word in the painting; Orpheus serenades rather than transfigures.[8]

Louise Nevelson continues to pack her transcendentally obsessive nostalgia for shipment; her vast boxed walls are like the contents of a gigantic warehouse where the ghost of Emily Dickenson is expected at any moment to claim the heirlooms of her fabled deprivations. But is it possible that a mortuary element is beginning, after repeated viewings, to overbear the spectral concreteness which has been Mrs. Nevelson's poetic lodestone? Curiously, the sense of a world embalmed appears to be furthered by her current use of gold paint, where before the wood-wedding world was marinated to mystery under Dickensian pall of black. But this is not the only reason for suspecting a fifth column of artistic termites in Mrs. Nevelson's mansion; her work, for these eyes, has begun to take on a quality of over possessiveness; it suggests the slightly skewed happiness of a keeper rather than a finder, the unsprung fancy of a poeticizing sensibility rather than the poetry of an ironic visionary. Mrs. Nevelson's sculpture has almost always depended on a kind of *curiosa felicitas* for its particular accent of success; its continued extension has brought it close to the paper moonshine of the patly bizarre.[9]

When Pater described the *Mona Lisa* or when Ruskin described the *Slave Ship,* they could begin by describing the "content" of the paintings and correlating these with the emotional responses of the critic. But if the painting is nonobjective and highly expressionist, and the artist intends to emphasize the spontaneous, physical aspects of the act of painting and, further, wishes to call attention chiefly to the material surface of the canvas, how should one go about describing and interpreting it? One can only experiment.

C)   But we wish to insist on the fact that in a full response to a work of art, there is an indissoluble residue of the personal. What is the claim of this assertion? Responses are personal. But if so, personal in contrast to what? Either something impersonal or something nonpersonal. The latter makes no sense. A nonpersonal response must be like that of a thing — sticks and stones and stars. It must be something purely mechanical in its influences and responses. But such things are objects and not persons, so how could they respond personally? On the other hand, human beings themselves must respond to works of art, as works of art — and this response must be that of a fully operative human being, conscious and sentient. In listening to a flood of sounds, a listener may use it as background music for his conversation and as a filler for the interstices of his mind. He is then using music rather than listening to it. For the latter operation, he must listen to it at all levels of his conscious being. The subjectivist may still be tempted to say: There still seems to be an element of the personal which cannot be pared away, for there is the subject, responding as a person. So it is plausible to say that the responses are not impersonal — that they are not impartial. This partiality cannot be removed. So all responses are on a par: they are all privileged. But will this line of argument bear scrutiny?

Our responses may be personal in the sense that we *own* our responses. Who else can feel for us? But from this statement, there is a great logical leap to saying that none of them can be impartial.

IV

Perhaps the lines of discussion I have been following—analyzing the idea of the unshareability of our subtle responses to works of art — is not what is implied in the claim that our responses to art are personal. What I mean is rather that my feeling in a certain way is no more justified than my feeling quite the other way. If I am bored at a performance of *The Firebird,* but no one else is, who is to say who is right? The ballet may have been danced with the lovely sets by Marc Chagall, and the firebird may have been Maria Tallchief herself, whose movements many critics find resilient and enlivening, clear and expressive in life. It is still indubitable that I was bored; though it may be that I am relatively inexperienced. Perhaps I am not familiar with the medium of the dance, or perhaps I do not know the tradition of this dance (never having seen Karsavina dance, let alone the other famous firebirds in the history of the ballet; Margot Fonteyn, Svetlana Beriosova, etc.). But somehow, I may think, the dancing of Tallchief seems cold, mechanical and purely technical. If the difference of opinion is between a relatively inexperienced person and someone who is highly experienced, we know where to place our confidence, though, naturally, mere experience is not enough for expertise. (A critic's expertise would not be fully credited if we knew that he is conservative, tradition-bound, or perfectionist; for example, Apollonian in his tastes, interested primarily in the formal technique and seldom impressed by expressive power or display of sheer will, energy and inner fire. To take another sort of example: a critic may be a fine expert, but if we knew that on the night of the performance, he was tired, ill or troubled, we would not give much weight to his judgment for that day; but there are critics who can overcome such diurnal irregularities in their work.) Even experts disagree. And when they agree in the decision, they frequently give incompatible reasons. All of this shows that the perception of the critics are personal — and one is no more right than the other.

The presupposition for the claim that there is no way of justifying one response over another needs to be examined very carefully here.

What is put into question is the response of the critics or ordinary viewers. We perceive works of art and feel about them in different and sometimes incompatible ways (in whatever way feelings may be incompatible). At the beginning of the disagreement, there is often a question of the descriptions and interpretations of the works of art. What tone was that? Was that an oboe that hit the wrong note? How is the tension-resolution of this movement brought about? Isn't this portion of this painting weak and ill conceived? Isn't the work of this novelist imitative? Many of these questions (not all) refer to particular feelings allied with bodily sensations. These features are relatively public and they are veridical. We ask each other about them. Some are also about mood features and the general characteristics of the work. Was it a tight and nervous performance? Is this a sad poem or a bitter one? Aren't the novels of Steinbeck sentimental, even when he puts on the pose of tough-mindedness? This painting, I think, is dizzying. The ambiguities in the word "feeling" which allows it to cover all of these examples shifts the issue finally to the question of how did you feel about it? which concerns the respondant's attitudes (likes and dislikes). Then we feel authorized to say that the responses of a perceiver are personal because people feel differently about works of art. To substantiate this divergence of opinion we offer as evidence such observations as "some people like this work, and others do not." "He enjoys the madrigals of Marenzio, but his wife does not." "He is very fond of the paintings of Murillo, even those of saccharine beggars." "He thinks the novels of John Steinbeck better than those by E. M. Forster." That is the way people feel, and they have these attitudes of favor and disfavor. To speak thus of attitudes of likes and dislikes seem plausible, but to say the same of the sorts of feelings that relate to bodily sensations and mood-features is less so. In any case, they are not unshareable or nonveridical. There is a logical muddle here. What is plausibly said of one sort of feeling, we tacitly shift and claim for feelings of another sort. While they are all feelings, and all of them certainly responses to works of art, they are not all alike. What particularly intensifies this confusion is the fact that people's enjoyment of works of art (what they take pleasure in) differs very widely.

There is not much more that needs to be added about the corrigibility of our descriptions and interpretations of works of art. In the rest of this chapter, I limit my discussion to our attitudes towards works of art; our approval, disapproval, our likings, dislikings and enjoyments. What I want to show is that (1) we cannot find a common attitude to be taken towards all works of art; and yet (2) there is still a sense in which the idea of justification can apply to the attitudes that may be formed toward them.

On the relational theory of value, the worth of works of art and all the emotional responses that flow from them emerges as a result of the interaction between an object and the perceiver. To put it another way, value is relative to such contexts. 'Relativism conceives of value as being an interaction between the object and the experiencing subject. One may refer to 'valued property' or say that values lie potentially in the object."[10] But from the fact that values are relational in this way, what may be inferred about the responses of the perceiver? (1) The values consist in and emerge out of the relation. (2) The relation itself is not a thing nor a property. So it must be an attitude on the part of the perceiver toward the object. (3) The value attitude may be treated as clues to or signs of the presence in the field of experience of objects of a certain sort. But clues and signs can frequently be misread or misunderstood. (4) The value relation is at least twofold. A perceiver must be present and his response must be registered; but so must the object of the *requisite* kind be present. In the absence of a work of art, no amount of relating will *in the long run* support a value claim. (5) Values do not exist *in vacuo*. Both attitudes of approval and revulsion are responses. But it is the work of art that must be valuable. And in this context, it is worth insisting that value is an attribute and thus adjectival and its use as a noun is a barbarism, though perhaps permitted by common speech. In any case, the cry that the value of a work of art must be relative because value is relational can amount to no more than the counter claim that objects of the requisite sort must be present.

Value is relational; it is an attitude. This tells us very little about what kinds of states of mind we are to assume. In the list of relevant attitudes, we find liking and disliking, approval and disapproval. But the question of the value of works of art, when asked properly, seems to be quite different. What is the value of *Oedipus Rex?* That is a question about the sort of merit and worth that the play has. Is *Oedipus Rex* pleasant? The play is too powerful, too overwhelming for that term. Do we enjoy it? Probably yes. It certainly is a great tragedy. But are tragedies the sort of thing that we enjoy? The answer is equivocal here. There are many works of art (Alban Berg's *Wozzeck,* the plays of Strindberg, the paintings of Bosch) for which saying that they are enjoyable seems to trivialize them. We willingly say that they are experiences; and we readily avow that such experiences are eminently worth undergoing. But pleasant? Enjoyable? They are not terms that seem to apply illuminatingly or relevantly. Not all works of art are pleasant, and we do not enjoy all works of art. The idea of pleasure or enjoyment cannot define the concept of a work of art.

Even if value is an attitude, it is not likely that our attitude to various works of art would be alike. What is the value of the *Odyssey?* What is the value of a Rembrandt self-portrait? The question seems queer. (It even sounds in the latter case like a financial question.) What are the merits of Homer's *Odyssey?* Compare the weaknesses of Virgil's *Aeneid* and Camões' *Lusiad* as epics. (The last reads like a typical examination question.) In each case the "values" and "weaknesses" are likely to be different; and our attitudes (whatever features they may have in common) are not likely to be the same either. I respond to the *Aeneid* and the *Ars Armatoria* of Ovid differently. My feelings do not even fall into the same species.

Nevertheless works of art form a class. And since all works of art are different, the common characteristics must lie in the fact of feeling as a response to them. The two candidates most often presented to describe this feeling are the "sense of beauty" and the "aesthetic emotion." Beauty in this context is usually defined as a species of pleasure — for example, objectified pleasure or disinterested pleasure.[11] To the extent that beauty is seen as a species of pleasure, part of my earlier comments about feeling and enjoyment is relevant to the issue here. But further, in the simple ordinary sense of the terms, beauty does not apply to all works of art, for there are many works of art which do not give us any pleasure. Not all works of art are beautiful, and in many, their ugliness is an essential feature of them. Neither is every beautiful thing a work of art. To say that a beautiful woman is a work of art is to make a joke, unless her beauty is artificial (but here the term "art" is being used loosely). Trees, vegetables and animals are often beautiful, but they are not works of art — unless God is seen as the supernatural artist. If we were to redefine the word "beautiful" to suit the problem here, the word "beautiful" would cease to be useful, for the notion of "beauty" becomes unfamiliar; and the language of art criticism takes on a remoteness from everyday experience.

While the word "beauty" has a perfectly common use, the word "aesthetic" is an invention of philosophers.[12] What is an aesthetic emotion? It must be either an emotion that we feel in the presence of beauty (this is not a likely usage) or the feeling that occurs in the presence of works of art. If the first is meant, the comments made in connection with "beauty" are applicable; and if the latter is meant, then it leaves open the question as to whether there is such an emotion; one which is familiar, comprehensible and uniquely common to works of art.

We use the phrases "aesthetic experience" and "aesthetic attitude" in connection with works of art. But I hope that it is now clear that they do not refer to any one special kind of feeling or event. The word "aesthetic" has many different uses. But if it means the sorts of attitude that we take towards works of art, then it is clearly not a matter of feeling nor any emotion, but a mode of apprehension. It is that attitude (stance) wherein we take our experiences immediately as pure sensory experiences; i.e., that in which we take what is presented to us for what it is. This usage coincides with the many technical uses to which the notion of the aesthetic has been put in the history of philosophy: e.g. the science of sensuous knowledge (Baumgarten); aesthetic intuition (Kant); the sense in which the aesthetic is the phenomenal given or our immediate experience (Hegel, C.I. Lewis); the sense in which the aesthetic is any experience unmediated by concepts (Kant, Kierkegaard).

How can we justify an attitude, a response that we make towards an object? If we were to think of the attitude on the analogy of pleasure, then it would seem that, on the evidence of experience, it would be difficult not to say that any response could be privileged. For, although our responses to objects fall within a range, the variations are astounding, and they are all legitimate. (At least this is what we would say of the pleasure responses of people.) But if we regard attitudinal responses in some other way, it might not be strange at all that there should be appropriate and inappropriate attitudes towards objects and events. Take the example of anger and resentment. In some contexts, anger is an appropriate reaction. In others, resentment rather than anger is the appropriate reaction. I may resent another person's inconsiderate, hasty judgment of my action. Often, however, anger may be unwarranted as a response. It would be unwarranted, for example, if the person knew the facts involved in my action but he was temperamentally unable to sympathize with me. Feeling guilty and feeling ashamed are suitable and proper in some contexts and not in others. A young lady who has elderly parents to take care of may feel guilty about wanting to leave home and have a career of her own, of developing her talents, of getting married and fulfilling her feminine hopes. While we may understand that her parents need her care and that she must remain at home, we may also think that she should not feel guilty or ashamed of her wishes; and it may be fitting for us to try to show her that she should not feel guilty; and if she does, she should try to reorganize her attitudinal patterns so that she should cease to feel guilty. It depends on the objective features of the context and the characteristics of the persons involved. On this basis psychiatric treatment often operates. Many of our guilts and shames are unrealistic and unwarranted; and we must try to remove them. In any case it makes sense to say that attitudes must fit the facts of the case. And the suitability of attitudes is not wholly a matter of arbitrary social norms. We can support an attitude which is not shared by our society and defend it, morally or from the viewpoint of utility. There are many cases in which we know that we should change our attitudes; we can assess their appropriateness, for ourselves as well as for others.

To shift to the aesthetic context: there are appropriate and inappropriate attitudinal responses to works of art. It would be odd to find an adequate performance of *Othello* amusing or to be terrified and frightened by a frothy, well-paced performance of *She stoops to Conquor*. To take a subtler case, it is an inadequate response to *Oedipus Rex* to find it only pathetic. However, the more common response, which is inappropriate, is to find a play, a film or a novel tragic, when it is merely pathetic or sad. We would say that most of the following are inappropriate: Levity as a response to the *Guernica*; whimsical amusement at the (what are really slightly sentimental) paintings of Picasso in his blue-tragic period. Frequently it is difficult to decide what the appropriate responses are: Is the *Dame aux Camélias* tragic or simply pathetic? Is this poem (by Hardy) bitter or sad? Is *Lolita* disgusting or is it high comedy? Or is it a clinical case study? These works of art subtly shade between a number of attitudes: bitter-sweet gaity, indulgent sadness, etc. The ambiguities are calculated and difficult to decide (though it must be emphasized that sometimes our inability to decide can be the result of our ineptitude). Though difficult to decide, some responses (e.g., to take *Lolita* as serious naturalism) are clearly wrong. And what is important here is the fact that, though we cannot say which responses are *the* right ones, we can say definitely which are wrong; for if we can say at any point that *this* response is inappropriate, then not all attitudes are permitted. While there are works of art about which we can be clear and certain, words to describe the attitudes may be difficult to find, as the appropriate words to describe our feeling evoked by the middle movement of Mozart's Piano Concerto in C-major (K.467). (In such cases, we often know better which adjectives do not apply than which ones do.) The appropriateness or inappropriateness depend on the nature of the case. No matter how chaotically we respond to works of art (surely not always the fault of the work of art) the objects themselves (if they have been structured with mastery) have determinable characteristics. They are not, like Rorschach tests, receptacles for whatever we wish to project into them. Nor do they, like mirrors, reflect whoever stares into them.

When experts disagree, it may be that both parties are wrong; or both may be partially right and partially wrong. The universe of art objects is "built up" from accumulated experience and judgments of many critical responses, and they constitute a class of objects (and entities) to which the majority of experts respond more or less alike. Time is a factor here — time for us to absorb them faithfully. We emphasize critical unanimity, though the interest and value of the unusual views (like Johnson's view of Shakespeare, Eliot's view of Milton) cannot be overlooked. To the extent that the experts are conscientious and free from the burden of *dead* tradition and conventionality, their expertise will be reliable. But there will always be works of art which will elude our understanding, and many works of art will rise and fall in critical and public affection (if not estimation). Critics are human after all, and they are subject to the stultification of their minds and the hardening of their critical skins. But that this condition should be permanent is not likely. The class of works of art is an open class. But there is a continuum from those works of art about which, throughout the ages, there has been un-animity of opinion to those about which there has been much dis-agreement.

There have been works about which there has been little question: Greek architecture and sculpture; the art of da Vinci and Michelangelo, some (though not all) of the music of Mozart and Beethoven, the novels of Tolstoy. Time does not seem to fade their merit but rather to add a glory to them. But there are works whose aspects make the universal appreciation of them difficult. Some feature or other of the following works have im-peded many people from appreciating them: many Renaissance madonnas, the paintings of Rembrandt, Baroque music, Shakes-peare (consider the attitude of the French throughout the ages; as well as the opinion of the English critics like Dryden and Pope), Rococo architecture and painting. Impartial judgments about them must not be always easy to form. Someone who did not like rosy cherubs and sweet madonnas might never succeed in *seeing* a Raphael accurately, and someone else might fail to appreciate that Rembrandt's aesthetic vision was ahead of his times. The work itself might be responsible for the absence of universal and spontaneous appreciation. Then there are works whose values fluctuate even more widely: Gothic architecture, the music of Gesualdo, mannerist paintings (Ribera, Andrea del Sarto, El Greco); Japanese woodcuts. All of these have features that are exaggerated, strong, accentuated — as art they posture. Historic-ally these works have shown great fluctuation as to the appre-ciation of them. But to the extent that we disagree over the merits of these works (after a careful and soul searching study), to that extent, they are not universal works of art (and perhaps inferior—

certainly limited in their appeal). The notion of universal appeal is (correctly or not) a part of the idea of art — and in our everyday convictions, we strongly believe that every human being, or most, when they carefully study and contemplate a work of art, will be rewarded by insight or enjoyment. Most works of art bear up under such intensive study. It makes no sense to say of great art that it will be exciting on first encounter, but will not bear close study and that it will begin to pall on subsequent encounter; nor does it make sense to speak of works of art which are permanently unappreciatable. It also makes no sense to speak of works of art which are "beautiful" to me but to no one else.

5 | THE OBJECTIVITY OF AESTHETIC JUDGMENTS

The value judgments that are formed in art criticism are to be thought of as the end of the activity. While the purpose of criticism is to come to an understanding of the work of art, the work of art itself is interesting to us because it is an object of value. In the process of trying to understand it, inevitably, we form an estimation of its worth and its place in the history of art. The judgments that we arrive at can take any of the following forms:

> Now the number of great works in the true concerto form is surprisingly small; far smaller than the number of true symphonies. And of this small collection a good two-thirds has been contributed by Mozart.[1]

> On any monument worthy of the name of monument the names of *Moll Flanders* and *Roxana,* at least, should be carved as deeply as the name of Defoe. They stand among the few English novels which we can call indisputably great.[2]

> The great English novelists are Jane Austen, George Eliot, Henry James and Joseph Conrad — to stop at that comparatively safe point in history.[3]

> For we know when we think of names like Giotto, Raphael, Titian, Rembrandt, Velazquez, that we are speaking of a class of

artists to which no English painter can possibly be supposed to belong. Even when we think of Poussin, Watteau, Ingres, Degas, we could only suggest one or two names as comparable; while Spain, Holland, and Belgium have each one name that we cannot parallel. [4]

I mean to exclude from this discussion judgments assessing the historical importance of an object of art, judgments of it viewed as an object of utility, or technical judgments such as the following: "The terra cotta Etruscan warrior at the Metropolitan Museum was 'made and fired in one piece, an achievement unequalled by any potter in modern times.' "[5]

The belief that judgments about the relative merits of a work of art are subjective is, of course, very old and very widespread. It has long been honored in the adage "De gustibus non disputandum est." More recently, it has been restated in the following way: aesthetic judgments are "employed, not to make statements of fact, but simply to express certain feelings and evoke a certain response. It follows," therefore, "that there is no sense in attributing objective validity to aesthetic judgment."[6] A critic says, "the *Marriage of Figaro* . . . is one of the supreme wonders achieved on the earth by human powers."[7] Such a statement according to Ayer is neither true nor false, since, though it obviously applies to the *Marriage of Figaro* in some general, unspecifiable way, it refers to nothing literally verifiable. It is noncognitive and at best expresses the enthusiasm of the speaker.

What is the nature of an aesthetic judgment? I attempt an answer by discussing what a value judgment commits me to; and this involves seeing just how the evaluation is related to the analysis, and how I estimate the justice and truth of evaluative judgments. There are important and crucial senses in which evaluative aesthetic judgments, like those above, are objective. I propose to show how this can be so and outline the limits of this objectivity.

I

I begin with an assertion of the sort that was given as an example. Suppose that a janitor or a bartender were to assert that a certain painting, to his knowledge, was one of the great paintings in the history of art. One would of course appreciate his sensibility but it would be wrong to put much credence in that particular pronouncement. If you took it seriously, it would be because you had heard these statements before, enunciated by people who ought to know. This example has a noncritical context. But it also happens that many people strolling in a museum might exclaim, "Oooh, isn't that wonderful? I like that. Don't you?" They are then expressing their delight; and if they were especially thoughtful, they could also pause and say, "I like that better than this," making an expression of preference.[8] I may be walking through a roomful of Dutch Masters with my little sister who stops before an incredibly sentimental genre painting and exclaims, "Oh, I like that!" Unless I were in an especially instructive mood, I would react in no special way except to lament, internally, this hereditary bad taste. For in such cases, I would know that she is simply voicing her little bits of unreflective pleasure. Even critics do this. There is no mistaking that, for they are creatures with emotions that can be triggered into activity by works of art. But if a critic were asked to say why he regards the items under consideration as outstanding, and he could not offer a word in explanation, that would be a disappointment! We might stare at the painting for a few minutes in an attempt to make it yield up its ineffable secrets; but ultimately we would conclude that the critic's assertions were empty — devoid of cash value; that they were a promise of enlightenment unfulfilled.

Both critical and noncritical contexts are alike in that with respect to either, one may ligitimately ask for "reasons." What the speaker says he likes may be anything: a painting, a poem, a dress, a plateful of fresh figs. Thus, one cannot separate the critical context from the noncritical by the sorts of objects claimed as an object of liking; nor can the two be separated because of the fact that in critical contexts, the "liking" and "evaluating" are backed up by reasons, whereas noncritical contexts are not, so that in the former it makes sense to ask why but not in the latter. In principle, one may ask "why" in both contexts and expect reasons. Either of the following conversations make sense.

  1. "I like north Italian cooking."
     "Why?"
     "Because it isn't so strongly flavored with tomatoes and oregano."

  2. "I like the paintings of Giovanni di Paolo.
     "Why?"
     "Because he created a convincing and imaginative world. And although he is 'often grotesque and sometimes rude,'

these faults come from his trying to express an inner spiritual strain which is still worth trying to express."[9]

We may sensibly ask "why" of judgments of "like" and "preference" when the taste expressed is unusual, eccentric, and we wish to have an explanation. The speaker may have special reasons for thinking that north Italian cooking is "better" than the usual sort of Sicilian cooking we encounter. Perhaps the speaker's great aunt (in whose house he grew up) had a superb Genoese cook. The difference between critical and noncritical contexts lies in this: in a critical context, the speaker is logically (or rationally) committed to giving reasons.

> 3. "I don't like dill pickles."
> "Why?"
> "I just don't, that's all."

> 4. "I don't like the music of Haydn."
> "Why?"
> "It is so jaunty and jangly that it gets me all nervous."

Noncritical contexts are those in which the speaker may legitimately refuse to give a reason *without* giving logical offense; or those in which if he does give a reason, it may be a peculiar, idiosyncratic (causal) reason of the sort that is unlikely to ever hold for anyone else. Such are reasons like the following: I don't like *Paradise Lost* because I was forced to read it by an English professor whom I hated. Or I like Rembrandt's portrait of his son because the luminous, sensitive eyes remind me of the eyes of my favorite cat. These are reasons, of course, but they are subjective, since they are biographical and personal.

Ordinarily, we signal noncritical contexts and reports of subjective preferences by the use of the verbs "like" and "please" or words such as "nice," "interesting," "pleasant". I like the voice of Maria Callas; the paintings of Grandma Moses are nice; the films of Ingmar Bergman are interesting and provocative. These terms are indicative of personal uses; and while it is still permissible for someone who hears such utterance to ask "why" or to contest such an assertion, to *insist* on an answer is a mistake. For the speaker does not commit himself to one.

> 5. "I found the depiction of Southern California derelicts by Steinbeck in *Cannery Row* very interesting. I liked that novel."
> "Oh, no! It is really quite a conventional, commonplace novel — most of the events are of the order of a day dream

75

and reveries; the prose style is self-conscious and a bit flabby; it has no nerve to it. It's not likeable at all. It is embarrassing to read."

It is possible to retort in this way, but we sound merely argumentative, in an unpleasant way. If on hearing the first remark, we were to ask why, and the speaker refused to say why except that he liked the novel, or simply mentioned some pleasant events in the novel that pleased him very much, we should not be surprised or offended. To insist on an explanation is to be rude: it is a breach of etiquette. For although the context may appear to be critical, the use of the terms "like" and "interesting" gives it a subjective twist. Though it may be a self-indulgent response, the speaker claims no universality.

In a critical context, on the other hand, critics, if they are critics worth their salt, must back up their assertion with some evidential considerations. We can regard critical assertions like "the great English novelists are Jane Austen, George Eliot, and Henry James . . ." as a promissory note, to take an analogy, which can be backed up by expert knowledge; and since the reasons are forthcoming, the judgments hold extrabiographical interest for us.

The use of the word "good" signals such objective contexts. That is one of the roles the term performs. "The novels of E. M. Forster seems to me to be very good. Even the earliest, journeyman works are very interesting and fine." The speaker is saying more than he liked them, if he did like them. (There are many works that we do not like, although we know they are good.) In employing this locution, he logically commits himself to offering considerations that would tend to show why the novels are fine. He may actualy find it difficult to offer the reasons required. For example, he may have felt very strongly that these novels are *good* and that considerations can be found to indicate why they are, but he may discover on trying to do so that he is not clever enough. If he says they are good, he is still committed to attempting to show why. (Of course he may not succeed; he may decide that the considerations that he can offer will not do at all; and that he has not considered the case well enough. He is not committed to succeeding. He may really be mistaken. But he *is* committed to trying.) If he is disinclined to give considerations or if he simply refuses to give them, he had no right to say the novels were good. He has misspoken. He ought to have been more cautious, more modest, and have said, "I like them" or "They are interesting to me." In saying that they were good, he has written a bad check. Terms like good, fine, worthwhile, in their objective uses, presuppose that the objects or experiences under consideration will be found to behave in similar ways for other people; that reasons can be offered to substantiate the claims made.

II

Art criticism and works of analyses are usually complex arguments. There would be no criticism, if the work of art did not render the activity worthwhile. The discussion assumes that the object discussed is a good work of art. The critic does not explicity draw the conclusion that it is a good work of art. After all, why discuss it if he does not think it is? Often the judgment is hinted at by the comparison that the critic makes. "We may reasonably, too, in the same way see some Dickensian influence in Conrad's use of melodrama, or what would have been melodrama in Dickens; for in Conrad the end is a total significance of a profoundly serious kind."[10] (There are cases, of course, in which a critic needs to reassess and devalue a portentous, major figure or a popular success by showing that the reputation is inflated. When the evaluation is negative, the critic is more likely to be explicit about it.) The whole discourse is an argument (or a series of them), because considerations are being offered for a judgment of a certain sort, and thus it is purposive. The analysis is an implicit process of reason-giving (wherein he mentions, primarily, those features of the work that are relevant to its understanding) and as a whole functions as the basis for the judgment (which is frequently unexpressed). The argument is complex because the features of the work of art that need to be indicated exist on several levels, and they require different modes of treatment. The critic needs to operate on all these levels, keep the strands distinct, and yet unify them.

The conclusion of the argument (if expressed) may be given either at the beginning or the end of the analysis. As it should be obvious, the analysis ought to be directed towards the understanding of the object before us, and the comprehension is related to the evaluation of the work: for an *understanding* of a work of art includes a cognition of its worth, in itself as well as in relation to other works like it. At a certain point in his essay on

"Flemish Art," Roger Fry[11] discusses Rubens' painting the *Martyrdom of St. Ursula.* He is in the process of determining and assessing the special characteristics of the art of Rubens and their significance in the history of art. There are a number of features, naturally, that Fry finds worthy of note, and he summarizes the influence of Rubens' predecessors (Carracci, Caravaggio) on him by saying, at the beginning of the discussion, that Rubens' significance lies in the creation of "one of the most perfect instruments of picturial expression that the world has ever seen."[12] What does it consist in? He particularizes it in two ways: first by discussing the features of the Baroque style, for Rubens had elaborated "them to the highest possibilities of expressiveness." But the crux of the discussion lies in the demonstration of these features in actual cases, showing that the generalization fits the particular cases, and also that the presence of these features constitutes the excellence, interest and the worth of the work. What he is saying is relevant to an understanding and appreciation of the work of art. Otherwise, the history that he brings to bear on the work would be irrelevant, even if true.

According to Fry, "one of the essentials of the Baroque style" is "the amplification and enlargement of the rhythmic phrase," and "a great increase of movement in depth; movement, that is, at right angles or diagonal to the picture plane and leading the eye back into the composition."[13] He proceeds to illustrate these features in a number of specific works. About the painting of St. Ursula he says, "I do not think that any of the pictures at Burlington House gave the full measure of Ruben's power in this respect [bravura of execution], but we may take the *Martyrdom of St. Ursula* as fairly exemplary."[14] Fry's stylistic generalizations have implicit in them a favorable evaluative judgment. The work in question it seems, is not in his opinion the best work to illustrate the artistic traits which account for Rubens' prominent position in the history of art. But apparently, it illustrates them well enough for present purposes.

> Here a great number of figures are shown in poses so instantaneous that none could have been studied by direct observation. Rubens had to rely upon his visual imagination with its stored-up knowledge of all the aspects of forms. And notice how perfectly all these forms fit into the turbulent rush of the rhythm, how definitely that rhythm is one of sequences of planes and not of lines, and how the diagonal movement into the depth of the picture space allows room for all this huddled confusion and gives it a harmonious unity. Note, too, the dramatic value given to the

figure of St. Ursula and the executioner who is on the point of cutting her down by making this a nodal point in the rhythmic theme, for here the main diagonal movement is sharply countered by St. Ursula's gesture as she is dragged down by the executioner to the left. This countermovement is again picked up to the right.[15]

Suppose we grant that the general statements about the Baroque style are warranted. How significant is their presence in this work? The demonstration must show not only that the features alleged are there but also that in this particular work, they are effectively present: that is, he must make us see (perhaps by argument but usually by pointing and by presentation) that there is a "bravura of execution" apparent, or a visible manifestation of Rubens' extraordinary feeling for volume and plasticity.[16] The features must be effective *in this case,* for it is obvious that the results of the presence of these features might happen to be, instead of bravura and plasticity, bombast, pomposity and busyness.

The analysis of the work, the pointing out of the features, the evaluation of the art are all inextricably interwined—and they are inseparable, for the very analysis leads to and warrants the evaluation. The analysis is either correct or incorrect; accurate or inaccurate; fair or unfair. Since the evaluative judgment is logically connected with the analysis, the value judgment, too, must be capable of being either correct, or incorrect, etc., depending on the worth of the analysis that backs it up. The usual discomfort that empiricists feel about this state of affairs reveals itself in the complaint that if an analysis is so closely tied up with a value judgment, the analysis must be noncognitive. What objectivity can an aesthetic judgment claim?

Suppose we were walking in a picture gallery and my companion who is an expert in Baroque painting paused before a Rubens and said, "This is the sort of thing Rubens used to do best, and he was a master at that!" Being interested (why else would I be there?) I might ask, "Why do you find Rubens so fine? I find his female figures fleshy and a little too exuberent." What I would expect then is a fairly detailed consideration of the painting. This is, in effect, what Fry is doing in the passages quoted (for although, we as readers do not have the painting before us, the essay itself was written as a lecture to be given at Burlington House on the occasion of an exhibition).

Fry discusses the unity in the color and tone composition, saying that the "unifying colours of light become as it were the dominant key of the colour scheme, and he suggests local colour by very slight variations from that."[17] We, as reader or listener, can check what he says, and our response should not be, "so this is how Fry feels" (which would be to imply that his remarks are subjective) but to ask, "It is true?" Much of the time Fry will be pointing out something which we had noticed already, but he will be indicating features and relations there which we might have failed to realize before. When he does so, we can decide for ourselves whether we gain anything from this new way of seeing and whether it is plausible or warranted.

One must notice that the facts cited are frequently about how we *respond* and how we *feel* towards a work of art, or how portions of it *appear to us*. We might, for example, say that a painting is restless or its movement is dizzying. These statements certainly constitute an emotional response. But whether it is subjective or objective is another question. "Looking at the press of martyred saints falling, we ourselves are not crowded or jostled." "The imagined movements which we are invited to make are everywhere free."[18] Stated in these ways the sentences have an objective function. They are open to verification, so that in these remarks we are not merely reporting a single's person's subjective responses. If it were so, the remarks would be stated more modestly: "The movement of shapes here *seems* crowded and turgid." (But if I go on to say, "I don't know whether they are or not. Are they?" then I am giving it an objective twist.) And it is open to us to treat this formulation objectively by replying, "Well, if it seems so to you, that is the way it seems to you, I suppose. But really they aren't. Look at the way colors have been used in pure patches here." The description is open to reinspection.

It is true that Fry refers to facts, but he also says that the forms "fit perfectly" into the turbulent rush of rhythm or that the unity is "harmonious." Are these statements not evaluative? To put the case even more strongly, can the critic ever avoid making appraisals and using appreciation terms? Fry in the passage quoted says "Notice how perfectly all these forms fit," and later on, "Note, too, the dramatic value given to the figure of St. Ursula." In the gallery, he might have said, "this is . . ." and pointed his finger. The presence of these indexical terms, indicating gestures and directive mode of speech deserve special attention. For by pointing out, the critic commends for special attention and thereby implies in this special way that the feature he is pointing out is worthy of notice. He would not point to any feature indiscriminately. What he points to is relevant to the task at hand, in the understanding, the appreciation and the evaluation of the work of art. He commends when he points, but that is not all he does. He is not *merely* evaluating or making visible a special interest and preference; there is an objective component in this activity. In pointing, he also indicates what there is to be seen. Pointing is not describing, though the words that accompany the gesture might be. But the gesture (the sign) has a reference; and for the gesture to be cognitively meaningful, the "object" of the sign must be ascertainable and present in some way. "This is an interesting feature," or "These forms cohere perfectly," or "This is worth watching" are suggestions to which one can agree and which, in some sense or other, are true or false. To quote other examples from Fry:

> Here the right-hand bottom part of the composition is in shadow, which is broadly contrasted with the bright light on the St. Ursula group.[19]

> And no less perfect is the setting: the gloom of the wood from which the Holy Family is emerging, the shimmer of moon light on the water.[20]

These descriptions are more or less accurate, depending on Fry's sensitivity in perceiving and on his skill in describing what he perceives faithfully; and they are helpful to the extent of our skill in guiding ourselves by what we hear and checking on what he says.

These activities, thus far, have some of the important earmarks of objectivity. In each instance, we, the recipients of the communication, can check on the reasons and ascertain for ourselves whether the critic is accurate or not and whether what he says is appropriate. We try to see what he sees and we can reject what he says sometimes. We might say, "You call this a swerving pattern. But isn't it true that this diagonal line and preponderance of black at the left hand corner are factors that break up the spiralling pattern and make the design of this painting static?" Reasons and features summoned up in this way are all corrigible and capable of reassessment. Further, the facts of reassessment and corrigibility presuppose, to a degree, the possibility of agreement. On these two counts, at least, aesthetic judgments are capable of objectivity.

Fry makes a number of very general historical statements which are worth commenting on. He says:

> Nothing is more remarkable about Rubens's art than the fact of his extraordinary feeling for volume and plasticity. We have seen again and again how inapt the Flemish, like all Northern peoples, were for such an imaginative comprehension of form, how instinctively they sought for flat linear descriptions of solid reality.[21]

It is possible to evaluate such historical generalizations on the principles of historiography. We may say that they are either correct or incorrect. But most of us do not know the facts of the case, nor have we a thorough enough knowledge of Flemish painting (or the art of the North) to be able to say whether the assertions are true or not. We also find general statements having to do with the principles and theory of color (in this case also partly historical) which are assessable in a similar way: "The early idea of colour harmony was of positive tints in certain proportions placed side by side. We saw that Metsys had already begun a more unified system by noticing a common influence on all the local colours which were subject to the same incident of light."[22] We can ask whether this is true. But we must also question its relevance to the task of appreciating those features that are worth noting in the work, features that define its special characteristics and which make them unique.

Sometimes the critic says that Rubens had a "marvelous power of visualization." He *mentions* what he wants us to see. This power, if Rubens has it, would be exemplified in a great portion of his work; it is a general feature of his imagination, but is it evident here in this case? How would one decide? The ability would show itself, partly in the following way: "whatever pose of a figure he might require, however improbable or extravagant it might be, he was able to bring to his inner vision an adequate and convincing image of it and project this on to the canvas."[23] Like a person's intelligence or sentimentality, this disposition would be more or less manifest in particular cases. Whether it is "marvelous" or not would depend on its strength in this case, though it would help to have other cases available for judgment. When someone says that something or other was "marvelous," "perfect," "powerful," "superb," he indicates a high degree of approval and enthusiasm, but the application of such terms are still assessable as regards their appropriateness. It would be a mistake to interpret them as simply instances of emoting (though it sometimes may be the most charitable thing to do).

82

It is obvious that various generalizations about works of art occur in art criticism. We may take them to be features of a work of art *to the extent* that these general properties are exemplified by the work under consideration. If they are not, then they are not features of the work of art. Many historical facts as well as biographical and sociological statements crop up in art criticism. Being general and often extraaesthetic, they cannot function as features of the work of art. They are useful in art criticism only to the extent that they aid us in the understanding of the work of art.

Aesthetic reasons are considerations about a work of art which are alleged to support an aesthetic judgment. The considerations, as I see them, must pertain to the work of art — i.e., they must be features of a work of art. Any feature of a work of art that may be relevantly mentioned in an analysis of it is a feature-reason, in some cases accurately and in others inaccurately alleged. To the extent that the act of analysis is logically complex (notice the multiplicity of the features that can be pointed out), feature-reasons are complex also, though all of them are alike in being corrigible and ascertainable. But not all the facts (i.e. features) related to a work of art can function as feature-reasons. It is a fact about the painting considered by Fry that it is by Rubens, and that its size is 0.48 x 0.37 cm., painted on wood; and that it was probably painted between 1620 and 1625.[24] They are facts *about* the work of art all right; but they cannot be reasons since they cannot relevantly function as a reason for an aesthetic judgment of that work of art. There are many such facts, but only some of them are features of a work of art (i.e., proferred as a reason in justifying an aesthetic evaluation). Alleged reasons are either good or bad. Good reasons are relevant reasons which are also true. Reasons may be bad, either because they are false or because, although true, they are irrelevant.

III

The aesthetic judgments I started to discuss were statements asserting that "such-and-such" is a great work of art. But most of the reasons given referred to its properties. In supposing that the latter in any way support the evaluative assertions, are we not making a mistake? It is usually believed that a value judgment cannot emerge from a set of descriptive statements. An *ought* cannot be derived from an *is*. We need, therefore, to look more closely at the relationship between the descriptions of a work of art and the evaluative assertions to see how they connect.

The clue lies in the word *assessment*. It is obvious that no single statement like "x is the case" by itself would ever show that Y, which possesses feature x, is thereby a good work of art. Our practice is always to mention a number of reasons in discussing a work of art, and of such a group of reasons some will probably be more important than others; but no partial list of them will ever serve to support the value judgment as well as all of them together. It seems to me that all the relevant features of a work of art, that is, all the possible reasons that can be given, all together, function as grounds for the assertion that such-and-such is a good work of art. If only some of the reasons are given, the assertion is only partially supported and the connection is left in doubt. Our response to such a partial list is that there is more to be said. This partial list may serve as a hint to a good observer to continue studying the work of art for himself. That the sum total of relevant features of a work of art serves as a basis for the final judgment is shown by the fact that a good critic is one who has taken into account all the facts of the case, i.e., all the relevant facts. Since all the facts, or as many as possible, need to be accounted for, the process of criticism is cumulative, and, in a sense, the job is always incomplete.

Sometimes a critic will be at a loss for words. He will begin to describe a work of art, but ultimately he must ask you to look at the object for yourself. He must ask you to do so either because he sometimes finds it difficult to verbalize what he sees or hears or because the work must make its own direct impact on you. A further reason is that only by direct confrontation can you open yourself to the total impact of the object. Works of art are unique, and their features are complex and difficult to describe. But if you look for yourself, you can see them. Since each feature of the work of art contributes to its uniqueness, each of them counts towards the final estimation. No one reason, or two or half a dozen, can wholly support an aesthetic judgment. All the relevant facts combined serve as grounds for our assertion. What we call assessment is this summing up in the light of our full knowledge and experiences stored up from the past.

Two objections may be raised at this point. (1) It is admitted that an evaluative conclusion cannot follow from nonevaluative statements, neither from a single one nor a limited set of them.

If this principle is correct, and a value conclusion cannot follow from a nonevaluative statement, then no more can it follow from a set of them, no matter how large, since a group of non-evaluative statements is still nonevaluative, and there is nothing magical in numbers.

Two different considerations bear on this objection. First, it is clear that although I have emphasized the objective aspect of the analysis of work of art — claiming that analyses are veridical and cognitive — it should be emphasized that it is nonevaluative (i.e., descriptively neutral) as well as evaluative. For when we analyze, all the while that we dissect, we make gestures of pointing, commending, with the presupposition that what we indicate is worthwhile attending to. There is also the emotionally heightened speech of synthetic interpretation. But how can something be both evaluative and descriptive? Even if these two modes are incompatible it cannot be wholly true of works of art, for they are objects of value. In dissecting such an object, is it surprising that what we say about them should be an admixture of both? In describing a work of art, we are trying to show what makes the object worthwhile — and what in it would repay study. (There are works of art, whose principal value is that they are pleasant and delightful, like Renoir's paintings of people on a pleasure boat, sun-drenched and sensuously rich. In discussing such a work, what we point out would be veridical, cognitive, and yet pleasant — and the sum total would show why Renoir's works are so highly admired. The value is inseparable from the description.)

2) Most of these so-called reasons must focus attention on the object of art itself, and all such reasons amount to saying that x is a good painting, a good poem or a good concerto because of what it is. If the reasons in such contexts refer to unique particular facts, the features that are referred to cannot be universally applicable. On the other hand, the logical feature of all reasons is that a reason that is good for one context must be good in any other like it.[25] For this is what makes a consideration offered, a genuine reason. And how can any consideration which has a reference to something which is unique and particular have universal application?

The principle suggested concerning the universalization of reasons, I believe, is sound. The answer to this objection comes in two parts. In principle, I do not see why any features mentioned should not be repeatable in other works of art. General features cited — life likeness of characters, etc — are of course repeatable. But so are arrangements of color tones, a certain handling of light, or a certain organization of elements. To be sure, we never expect a complete duplication of elements, exactly arranged in the same way, for we find that features in a work of art change their character due to their context and they influence each other. This, however, does not preclude the repeatability of various features. (It is because they *are* repeatable that it is possible to talk of *types* in the arts.)

On the other hand, the uniqueness of a work of art and the dependence of the character of a feature on the rest of the work of which it is a part mean that there will always be relevant dissimilarities between any two works of art, and this I believe is enough to suspend the requirement of universalizability. For the principle of universalizability of reasons must include in its statement that when there are relevant differences, the reasons need not (and indeed cannot) be transferred from case to case. To the extent that there are always relevant differences (and in works of art, this extent is considerably large) this principle becomes of less importance, though it is still true. (That much of our reason-giving is done by means of pointing — what one saves by pointing is a minute description — frequently conceals the complexity of works of art, and their relevant dissimilarities.)

I am at this point uncomfortable about my description of the connection between an evaluative judment and reasons given to support it. (I reopen the question in the next chapter.) I seem to be saying the following: indeed one *can* defend the evaluation placed on a work of art by giving all the relevant reasons for it, but since this class of reasons is large and subtle, or difficult to verbalize, what is theoretically possible (if it is) is practically impossible. You can seldom, if ever, realize it. But to say this seems to make the justification of an aesthetic judgment impossible in practice and the objectivity of aesthetic judgments an illusion. We can try to avoid this stalemate by reminding ourselves that there are better and poorer jobs of criticism. If we can make this discrimination, talk about works of art is not wholly futile. We need to get a proper view of the logical nature of aesthetic arguments and reasons. It should be clear from what has been said so far that to think of the model of such arguments as being either deductive or inductive is erroneous.

A number of phenomena in the critical activity may be explained on the basis of what I have said. A positive, favorable evaluation is grounded on the cumulative effect of taking into account a whole range of reasons, and therefore it is very difficult for critics to support, in a few words, an assertion like that made by Leavis: "The great English novelists are Jane Austen, George Eliot, and . . ." A large number of considerations must go to support a conclusion of that sort. Dr. Leavis needed a whole book to attempt to do so, and whether he succeeded in doing so still remains an open question. The dialectic of the book was a detailed consideration of the novels of these writers and was intended to make a case for this bold and astounding assertion. Leavis' statement is a sweeping generalization. But the same is true of more modest proposals. A particular assertion such as "This painting by Rubens is a good painting" is as difficult to prove as the previous example because of the multiplicity of reasons and their complex interrelationship. Sometimes we are at a loss to decide what features to point out because the organic synthesis of all the characteristics of the work of art constitutes its excellence.

At the same time we find it easier to show conclusively that a work of art is defective. All one needs to do is point out detrimental features, and a limited set of reasons can do this. An example is Tovey's argument that Beethoven made a mistake in introducing a change in tonality within the opening statement of the ritornello in the first movement of the First and Third piano concerti.[26] If Tovey's arguments are correct, then this argument is enough; and we can definitely tell the conclusion follows. Such a demonstration can be done simply and more directly than the contrary job of mustering arguments to show that an object is admirable. We can say that *because* of feature x, this work is not very good; but we can never say that *because* of feature x, this work of art is good.

The critical situation is complicated; and in a world where absolutely perfect things are few, there are many works of art which contain flaws. *Hamlet* retains a high status as a tragedy despite numerous negative criticisms made of it, ranging from the triviality or inconsistency in Hamlet's motivation to faults in the versification.[27] T. S. Eliot says that "probably more people

87

have thought *Hamlet* a work of art because they found it interesting, than have found it interesting because it is a work of
art."[28] Were we, despite Mr. Eliot, to attempt to argue for its
high status, then either we must show that what are reputed to be
flaws are not really flaws at all, or show that there are overriding
considerations which compensate for these flaws. This is to say
that sometimes we can show that a reason given is wrong.
Reasons may be falsified in a number of ways. A feature which
has been mentioned may not really be there. Or it may have been
seen (or estimated) erroneously, and we can suggest a more accurate, richer way of regarding the features under consideration.
Is the Freudian explanation of Hamlet's relation to his mother
(and indirectly to Claudius) accurate? We can look at the play
again to see whether there is anything to support this interpretation, either in the words or the actions of the play. Or lacking
this direct way, we may construct a better account, one which is
more direct, less speculative and more faithful to the text, to explain Hamlet's procrastination. Thereby we reject certain reasons
given because we think they are irrelevant to our attempt to
understand the work of art; and because it is unnecessary to the
understanding of the work of art, it is also unneccessary in its
evaluation. We sometimes say that considerations of size in
painting, subject matter in poetry or conventional morality in
the novel are, in this way, irrelevant. If they are, what I have
said explains why.

IV

I have presupposed all along that we will attempt to give only
reasons that are relevant in justifying aesthetic judgments. But
what can be said about the criterion of relevance? In the process
of reason-giving, we only mention (or mean to mention) factors
that are relevant to the argument. So we do not mention everything that is true about a work of art: size in painting,[29] or the
length of a poem, for example. Then in what does the relevance
of reasons consist? How do we know whether any fact indicated
is relevant?

According to an important traditional account, a reason is
relevant if a feature pointed out is a characteristic that defines the
genre to which the work belongs: for example tragedy, epic
poetry, sonnet, *opera seria*, classical concerto, etc. I mention this
theory here to indicate the role that, on some views, the notion

of genre plays in the logic of objectivity. I do not think that this answer is adequate; but I shall discuss it in detail later.

Something still needs to be said about the idea of relevance — not the criteria of relevance. Are the reasons that any critic gives in any way relevant if the judgment precedes the reason-giving? One feels that often the critic does not have the considerations he offers in mind when he decides. He looks at the work of art or listens to the music; and perhaps because of his experience or intuitive acumen, he effortlessly makes the right judgment. Then he looks over the work again, listens to the music, to look for likely justifications. But none of these really had anything to do with the *making* of the judgment. They are really irrelevent to it because he was not thinking about them when he decided.

That state of affairs is probably typical of many critics in the arts as well as of many other experts: hospital inspectors, production managers, efficiency experts in the factories, etc. They look over the institution they are expected to improve; and because of their knowledge and experience, they catch the ambience of the place and can diagnose the ills within a short while. Having decided what the ill must be, then they go about looking for it; or otherwise look for the justification of what had been decided. (An experienced philosopher, reading over an essay, intuitively knows that something is wrong and then sets about to give reasons for it by reading the essay again, combing the logic, etc.) But in all these examples, the reasons given are all really afterthoughts: the judgment was arrived at in another way. The difference between an expert and an amateur connoisseur is that the expert can fish for and find likely reasons, whereas the amateur can make the right judgment but often cannot find the reasons to go with it. In a way, what the experts seem to have over the amateurs is a verbal facility. The reasons given constitute an *expost facto* justification of opinion rendered.

This *post hoc* mode of justification is typical of many states of affairs: but the idea of relevance emphasized by such a mode of argumentation seems to be some form of psychological relevance, usually a causal factor. However, if the critic first decides in what appears to be an intuitive manner, and then looks for reasons, the reasons seem not to be functioning even in a psychologically relevant fashion, unless we are willing to say that the reasons operated unconsciously. As a conscious causal factor, it is clear that the reasons are not relevant, for they follow rather than precede the decision. It may even be that what *did* relevantly function in forming the judgment is not even mentioned among the reasons that the critic gives.

In this study, however, the relevance in question is a logical relevance. We are concerned with reasons that logically support the judgment and if they logically support it, then they serve their purpose, whether they were present in the mind of the critic before the assertion of the judgment, at the time of it, or came to him only long after the pronouncement. What is psychologically relevant can be legion, the human nature of critics being very diverse. But if the reasons are logically relevant, then they would be so for any critic. If it is correctly asserted that reasons x, y, and z are relevant to judgment P, then they would be so for any other critic, A, B or C, barring prejudice, myopia or a fundamental disagreement on the nature and definition of art.[30] (Of course, this is not to say that reasons x, y, and z, which relevantly support judgment P, would also support judgment Q, no matter how much alike P and Q are. In crucial cases the uniqueness of works of art (as mentioned in a previous section) rule out x, y, z. The relevance refers to the logical connection between judgment P and reasons x, y and z. *This* is not a psychological connection.)

If the reasons are logically relevant, then they would be relevant no matter what the conditions under which they are enunciated: even in such extreme conditions as when a critic first asserts them in ignorance or unwittingly. Later on, he will see that he gave the right reasons. We cannot require that the logically relevant reasons be present in the mind of the critics temporally before the formation of the judgment. To insist on this is to think of the formulation of the judgment as a process of subsumption or categorization: reasons x, y, z apply, so object K must be so-and-so. The formation of aesthetic judgments does not necessarily proceed in this manner. Reasons are possible. But they do not arise mechanically, nor do we apply pre-established categories formed in the abstract.

V

Still critics disagree about the relative merits of a work of art, and surely, one might insist, this shows that an aesthetic judgment is always subjective. The apparent relativity of aesthetic judgments (which we say can be shown by the disagreement among critics) has been traditionally the strongest argument in support of the subjectivity of aesthetic judgments.

The disagreement may be viewed in two ways though both amount to the same thing. (a) Two critics can give the same description of an object but emerge with different evaluations. Or (b) they view two objects in the same way but grade them differently. We must mean that either of these is the case when a person says of taste that there is no arguing about it because taste differs so. We must be talking about the *same* thing. For example, any two of us can agree about the characteristics of *Pride and Prejudice;* (all of them, their meanings in the context of the novel, the merits and demerits of these features as well as what criteria are relevantly applied to *this sort* of novel, etc.); we agree about all of these; and I say it is a superb novel, and you say I overestimate it. It is still open to me to like or dislike a work of art which I evaluate aesthetically in a certain way, for there is no contradiction in saying, "I like *Pride and Prejudice* though *Emma* is the better novel. I like it better than *Emma.*" (Such a statement is frequently made.)[31] If the objects under scrutiny are different or are evaluated with different gradings, then the discovery that people's opinions about them differ would certainly come as no surprise. The assertion that aesthetic judgments are subjective is interesting only because we assume that two critics can be faced with (can confront themselves with) the identical object. They see the same painting or groups of paintings, hear the same performance of the same musical compositions, etc. They describe the works in the same way, but they emerge with different evaluations (good or bad). This is assumed even in more general assertions about the difference of taste, as when we say Berenson values Italian paintings of a certain sort; Clive Bell ranks higher paintings of quite another sort. Both are experts; and doesn't this show that taste again can differ? We find such differences interesting because we assume that, standing before a group of cubist canvases, Berenson could see more or less what Clive Bell could see. If he didn't or couldn't, then his not agreeing with Bell about the merits of modern painting is not surprising, nor does the assertion about the subjectivity of aesthetic judgments necessarily follow.

The assertion that aesthetic judgments are subjective thus presupposes that when two critics make two incompatible value estimations, these are grounded on an agreement about the analysis and interpretation of the work of art. At least they must not differ radically about the facts of the case. While we certainly believe that people see and experience things in much the same way, when a difference of evaluation arises, we assume readily that first of all the difference must be due to a discoverable difference in view point.

The basic presupposition which underlies the whole of critical enterprise seems to me that (1) works of art can be understood and mastered on their own. (2) It is possible for two critics to agree about the characteristics, the nature, of a particular work of art. (3) And the whole logic of criticism presupposes that the reasons proffered for an aesthetic judgment are mutually corrigible and reassessable. The very fact that these presuppositions are made leads people to say that there is (or may be) an element of taste in critical judgment; and it is revealing that this rock-bed of objectivity should lie under the dictim of subjectivity.

I say that this objectivity is "presupposed." Without it, the whole activity of criticism is impossible. Is it a correct presupposition? I believe that it is borne out by experience; but one part of it seems to me a matter for empirical study, and the other part is a problem for general aesthetics — to provide an answer to the question "What is the nature of a work of art?" In our pessimistic mood, we notice the chaotic state of criticism. But what, after all, do we wish to establish when we say that there is an element of taste in all aesthetic evaluation? We want to point out, perhaps, that there is a residue of fundamental difference in the way that critics respond to a work of art. They see the same groups of objects, describe, analyze and interpret them in the same way and still respond in incompatible ways (though I leave unspecified the respects in which such responses may be incompatible). We must exclude cases in which the response is purely personal, as when a critic says: "Yes, Van Gogh is a good painter — not as great as Cezanne, but nevertheless he is a master. However, I do not like him. He makes me feel ill-at-ease." There may even be differences of opinion in expertise, a famous example being the now ancient quarrel over Milton between T. S. Eliot and the rest of the critical world. Yet the critics considered Eliot's reasons (as if to say that his reasons *were* somehow relevant to the case) and many concluded that Eliot was wrong. No matter how discordant critical statements are, critics themselves seem disinclined in their work habits to ignore them.

VI

The very statement "aesthetic evaluate judgments are nonobjective" presupposes an element of objectivity. In making this assertion, we usually mean that when two critics have come to an adequate cognition and understanding of an object of art, even when this cognition is similar in all important aspects, they may emerge from this experience with two different (incompatible) judgments. Unless we recognize that there is this similarity of cognition and incompatibility of judgment, we cannot say the judgments are relative. So we presuppose, first of all, that we experience works of art in fairly similar ways and our comprehension of works of art are mutually corrigible. This is one mode of objectivity.

We further assume that a critic will say a number of things that logically relate to this judgment. What he says in the analysis and interpretation backs up the judgment. The two are in some sense logically related. And since things he mentions are features of the work of art, all of them are publicly inspectable. Therefore, this is another mode of objectivity.

It is difficult to say anything very illuminating or very definite about the criteria of relevance. But whatever we do say about them is conditioned by a number of beliefs held in general aesthetics. Works of art are autonomous. We must take them also as objects that are unique and particular. They are objects of concrete sensuous embodiment. If these statements are true, then in crucial cases it is impossible to subsume a work of art under universal principles. For what reason counts as a good reason for backing up an aesthetic judgment seems to depend on the nature of the particular object we have before us. And for that there will be no established rules or principles. The criteria of relevance then hinge on this aspect of the nature (or definition) of a work of art.

Does this make criticism seem impossible? Not at all — though it does make it difficult. That it is hard to talk meaningfully and sensibly about works of art is a well-known fact. Fortunately, there have been many fine critics and good works of criticism to dispel the gloom of despair. To say that they are *good* works of criticism means, among other things, that they have passed the test, up to now, of countless re-examinations.

6 | AESTHETIC REASONS

When we argue, we exchange reasons. Whatever a critic says, we want to know why he says it. What considerations could he offer? "Although much can be said in praise of the National Gallery Virgin of the Rocks, it falls far short of the Louvre picture in every kind of beauty."[1] "Puccini was 'an artist who bore the authentic stamp of genius but who for some reason failed to cross the boundry into the realm of absolute greatness.' "[2] Even when we agree with the critic (though particularly when we do not agree with him), we want to know what he can do to substantiate his claims. We want to be given some reasons — some standards, considerations, conditions, criteria — which we can clearly and unequivocably apply in order to reach the conclusion. We have in mind a number of different models of argumentation. (1) Other things being equal, we want the considerations to function as necessary conditions for the application of the claim. (2) Or we want the considerations all together (a set of them being given) to be such as to enable us to say that because of features x, y, z . . . object P qualifies for the appropriate evaluation. (3) Even if we did not exact such a rigorous scheme for aesthetic arguments, we may still want a set of conditions which, other overriding factors not interfering, would at least cumulatively count towards a decision. Such conditions[3] (called defeasible) are neither necessary nor, as a set, sufficient; but they are nevertheless criteria to be applied. A set of defeasible con-

94

ditions is not sufficient because for any such list, there is always another open list of defeating conditions. That is, an object with features w, x, y and z . . . would fall into a category P unless that object has another feature or two which would overrule the application of the standards.

But can any of these schemes of argumentation and reason-giving make sense in talk about art? Many people have answered that question in the negative. To begin with, we seem not to be able to formulate the standards or criteria. This in itself is a major difficulty. But further, many aesthetic concepts seem not to be condition-governed. (See Chapter 3, III.) A set of factors that makes a sequence of frames in one film taunt, dynamic and expressive (all aesthetic properties) may not produce the same results in another context. Finally, a number of philosophers, chief among them Kant and Croce, have argued that no concepts, genres nor universal categories may be generated from works of art. If this is true, then we cannot base any set of standards on the criteria that constitute the category or genre. We seem to have destroyed the chief model we have for aesthetic arguments. (This consideration was elaborated in the preceding chapter.)

What are aesthetic arguments like?

I

It is true that in all modes of reason-giving, we present considerations which must serve as reasons in other relevantly similar cases. If factors x, y, and z are offered as reasons to support proposition P, then they must also be capable of supporting proposition Q which is like P in relevant ways. If they apply to one case but not the other, we must take care to show why they fail to apply in the one case. We may do so by showing some dissimilarity between P and Q or pointing out the presence of some factor in Q which negated the applicability of x, y, and z as support. To do this, however, is to show that had things been equal, x, y, and z would be reasons for Q. Otherwise, the reasons given (i.e. x, y, and z) would, to begin with, explain nothing of P.

The range of the application of the principle of the universalizability of reasons is very wide. If an argument is valid because its form is the disjunctive syllogism, then any other argument of a similar form must be valid. If this were not so, how could we say that the original argument was valid *because* its form was that of the disjunctive syllogism? In another example, if Jones were liable to prosecution because of the violation of a certain law, then any other individual (relevantly specified) who broke the same law would likewise be liable to prosecution. This is how legal reasoning goes. The application of criteria in various grading activity proceeds in similar fashion. The criteria for stamping eggs as grade A, beef as prime, or Assam tea as first quality apply to all other entities of the same class. The principle applies not only to justifying reasons but also to causal reasons. We may wish to explain the occurrence of A by pointing out B as its cause, or factors 1, m, n, o, which together constitute B. But if on another occasion, when B is present, we do not find A, could we have found the adequate cause of A in the first instance? Or if on a third occasion, we should discover that A is present yet B did not come about, we would feel that the cause had eluded us. Before we accepted this chaotic state, we should like an account of the extenuating factors that would explain the failures of the causal sequences. But to do so is to seek universalizable causal reasons. The universalizability of causal reasons has been their prevalent feature since the writing of Hume's *Treatise*.

While all reasons are universalizable, there are apparently two sorts possible: those which are based on a general statement (type-U) and those which mention in the statement, an individual person or condition (type-E).[4] Reasons of type-U, of which moral reasons are the primary examples given by Hare, are clearly universalizable. For example: if John's treatment of Mary, his wife, is immoral because it really is a form of self-aggrandizement (however this complex relation is to be characterized), then any-one else's treatment of another person, where the relationship and the manner of treatment were relevantly alike, is likewise immoral. There is another way of describing the universalization of moral principles. This is the Kantian formulation: an action is moral to the extent that its maxim or principle (whatever it may be) is one that we would be willing to have anyone else, in a relevantly similar position, act on. If we are not willing to do so, we are making an exception of ourselves; and this is immoral unless one can show why we are different from other people. (This last condition itself is in accordance with the principle of universalization.)

What of reasons of type-E? Hare agrees that a reason cannot be a reason for *this* (particular) occasion only.[5] Yet any reason that mentions a specific person, time or place cannot simply be made to apply to other persons, times or places. Then how could type-E reasons be said to work? It would be worth looking briefly at an instance of a type-E reason, a historical explanation.

> Why was Julius Caesar assassinated?

> He was assassinated because he violated the sovereignty of the senatorial order. The noble senators would not resign without a battle the privileges which their order had enjoyed for centuries.[6]

The individual mentioned may be any individual — a person, a time, a place. This argument refers specifically to the character of a particular group of persons (among them Brutus, Cassius, etc.) and when we place them in a specific time and place, Rome in 44 B.C., we have a complex event but one which is unique in history. How do these type-E explanations manage to elucidate? They indicate various factors, the absence of which would have probably changed the course of events. This event is a concrete event. But the significance of the features we point out — like the character of Brutus and Cassius, the economic interests of the senatorial class, though related to particular persons, a particular place, at a particular time, are still further grounded on many lawlike propositions which hold in other relevant cases. The proper names, the time and place, are, in a way, shorthand for the character traits of the men involved, or various repeatable geographical and economic truths. If the events were unique, citing them would explain nothing. It would be like saying that X happened because of Julius Caesar, but nothing has been or will be like him because he is unique. As an explanation, this is unilluminating. Thus, even type-E reasons when examined closely are grounded on (backed up by) type-U judgments that serve as presuppositions. The world is made up of particular individuals, but fortunately, they fall into various categories and patterns. This is the logic of historical explanations, developed in accordance with the account of reasons given above.

II

There is an initial attractiveness to the view that reasons are universal and repeatable in art criticism, because there are many examples that fit this description.

Reasons that apply to a whole class of entities can be produced to the extent that there are genres (or forms) and these genres are governed by principles of conventions. The class may be defined by way of a form (like the sonnet, detective fiction, tragedy, the classical symphony) or a group of things created within a historical period.

> [Mendelssohn's] Violin Concerto thus became the original type of the majority of modern concertos; and being, as it is, an original inspiration, it is far greater than any work that has ever followed its tradition.[7]

> Caylus has been derided for saying that [Watteau] was deficient in the art of composition; but from the academic point of view, he was right. Watteau never mastered the baroque trick of relating figures in depth. In his large pictures the groups are dotted about in rows, with a backcloth behind them; only in his small pictures, where all the figures are in the same plane, is there a perfect feeling of unity.[8]

> So slowly does the action move that it seems more like a sequence of ecstatic stillnesses without progression or tension. Reading this "remembrance of things past" we feel convinced that the permissible measure of slowness is overstepped. Plot there is almost none; and not a whit of dramatic interest. Thus the novel is reduced to pure motionless description, and the diffuse, atmospheric character, which is in fact essential to the genre, appears with exaggerated purity.[9]

Eternal genres may not exist as they would in Plato's heaven; but many works of art fall into types, displaying similar features and there is no harm done in grouping them. Any principle that one might be able to generate from a study of such groups would, of course, be only generally applicable; but it is, at least, a weak criterion.

If the categories are dead, no longer practiced (such as the baroque cantata, Greek tragedy, the classical concerto), then, there is no reason why fairly strict generalizations cannot be formulated, provided literary historians and critics utilize their ingenuity sufficiently. A case in point may be Tovey's discussion of the classical symphony and the concerto.

When artists work within a vigorous tradition, carefully guided by precedent, or belong to an active and closely knit school, the works that they produce are bound to have features that resemble each other. Such resemblances, formulated into a principle, would form a canon.

> And I would suggest that the difference between that modern poetry which we feel to be in the main stream of great art and that which, however attractive or startling, seems to be pursuing a byway or a backwater, may lie in the following or the forsaking of the paths shown by this age-old and almost eternal môlpe.[10]

> Chiyo . . . was a true poet, but not a haiku master. Her finest
> poem . . . is pure poignant emotion, and if it is "not haiku",
> it is simply in the sense that English is not Greek: they are
> different languages.[11]

In the teaching of some quasi-evaluative terms (I can show this best by the case of negative terms) the reasons we offer are frequently of general nature. Here are two examples: (a) This is sentimental because it is the display of more emotion than the situation warrants, and we can see that the author has been "blinded by his own warm tears." Further, the sentimentality of this passage is betrayed in the word choice which is "too archaic— that is, too poetic." Where what he says "should be strictly controlled by the emotions that is being expressed, he has slipped into a literary habit."[12] (b) The organization of the opening tutti is ineffective because he fails to perform the requisite key changes.[13] In both of these cases, the critic would probably indicate other works to reinforce his lesson.

Sometimes a general theory of art can be applied to a specific case. One might say that this is a good poem because "a good poem is the expression of emotion; in a bad poem, expression fails." Tolstoy says that "almost all the chamber and opera music of our times — beginning especially with Beethoven" is bad art, for "by its subject matter, [it is] devoted to the expression of feelings accessible only to the people who have developed in themselves an unhealthy nervous irritation evoked by this exclusive, artificial, and complex music."[14] He also says that Beethoven's Ninth Symphony is bad art because it has not "the quality of uniting all men in one common feeling." The "feelings transmitted by this work could [not] unite people not specially trained to submit themselves to its complex hypnotism."[15] It is not Christian universal art. These reasons are difficult to assess since their cogency depends on the correctness of the general theory.

All of these are actual cases of aesthetic reasons; and they cite some general principles or criteria. It is the presence or absence of these features which make the difference between the success or the failure of the object. In each instance, the case is made to the extent that the reason proffered is true of the work cited; but the examples are, from the viewpoint of a work of art, special, for in none of them can we extend the pattern of argument much further.

One would suppose that an aesthetic reason is relevant if a feature pointed out is a characteristic that defines the genre to which the work belongs. That there are such genre is undisputed. A clinical discussion of one such literary genre, the tragedy, was closely developed by Aristotle. The usual interpretation of the *Poetics* is that he has formulated a set of principles or canons for tragedy. A good tragedy is one which displays all or most of certain criteria: and valid reasons for judging a play to be a satisfactory tragedy must refer to one of these criteria-features. When one examines more closely the implicitly presupposed logic of genre, one can see that this account cannot be correct.

Recent discussions of the nature of tragedy, especially in relation to plays like the *Death of a Salesman,* offer a convenient starting point. An important criticism of the play has been that Willy Loman does not succeed in rousing the sympathy of the audience; whereas in order to excite pity and fear, a hero must be, in Aristotle's words,

> a man not preeminently virtuous and just, whose misfortune, however, is brought upon him, not by vice and depravity but by some error of judgment, of the number of those in the enjoyment of great reputation and prosperity,

and he goes on to say

> The perfect Plot, accordingly, must have a single, and not (as some tell us) a double issue; the change in the hero's fortune must be not from misery to happiness, but on the contrary from happiness to misery; and the cause of it must lie not in any depravity, but in some great error on his part; the man himself being either such as we have described, or better, not worse than that.[16]

Is our objection to the *Death of a Salesman* a fair enough criticism? First of all one must decide whether, as a matter of fact, Willy Loman fails to excite pity and fear. Does he perhaps merely arouse pathos, indifference or irritation? Suppose we agree, for the sake of the argument that Willy Loman only provokes irritation. Even so, we might be able to avert that criticism if we could discover that the play is not really about Willy Loman. Might not the tragedy be about someone else or something else? It is because the main protagonist of the play *is* Willy Loman and he does not arouse in some of us any pity or sympathy (though probably fear)[17] that the following last ditch defense of the play was voiced: that Willy Loman is a tragic hero because he is endowed with an "inherent unwillingness to remain passive in the face of what he conceives to be a challenge to his dignity, his image of his rightful status. Only the passive, only those who accept their lot without active retaliation, are 'flawless.' Most of us are in that category."[18] The play, says Miller, is a tragic play because it moves us as all tragedies do, from the

> fear of being displaced, the disaster inherent in being torn away from our chosen image of what and who we are in this world. Among us today this fear is as strong, and perhaps stronger, than it ever was. In fact, it is the common man who knows this fear best.[19]

Well, is this defense just or not? It is clear that Arthur Miller is asking for a new norm for the tragedy, and he is saying that while Aristotle's canons are adequate for Sophocles and perhaps even for *Othello* and *Coriolanus,* they are not appropriate for the modern stage, A criticism which is relevant to the one is not necessarily relevant to the rest despite the fact that they are all called "tragedy." We must learn to see (and respond) to these new plays in a new way.

All this is, in a sense, a critical issue rather than a logical one. But the issue is wholly complicated by the fact that at any moment the genres that we have are ill-defined, and further by the fact that they are continually being changed, created and discarded. To amplify this point: works of art only occasionally come bearing the labels of their genre. Perhaps they usually do in music, but less so in literature, and least of all in painting and drawing.[20] Therefore one has to guess whether they are intended to fall into a genre, whether they do so or not, even apart from what was intended, and what the genre is. And even so, one has them in an ill-defined and changing group.

Once the members of a genre have been decided on, general descriptions of it can be formulated inductively. A new class in an art may be generated by external stimuli. A discovery in some other area of human activity may prompt artists to formulate a new theory about reality, or extend the range of the subject matter and form of art, etc., and create new genres. Examples could be the rules of impressionist paintings, based on a theory of light and color or the relations between Freudian psychology and surrealism. Critics and art historians may manage to agree about these rules and many artists may continue to work within them. But there will always be artists who will deliberately go about testing these rules, stretching them to the extreme, frequently violating them. The very restraint imposed by these rules seems to goad them to break out of them, to show the world that human creativity transcends rules and that a satisfactory work of art could be produced which is not subject to them.

One has only to recall the disagreement on standards that took place when Wordsworth wrote his "Preface to the Lyrical Ballads"; again in the controversy over free verse; and even more recently in certain quarters over the poetry of Ezra Pound. We have other familiar cases in the initial rage against the fauvist and cubist painters early in this century and, more recently, the traditionalists' abuse of the works of the abstract expressionists and action painters or the pop and op artists. In each case, there was the denial that these were works of art. The reasonable view to take, however, is that we must have different sets of criteria of relevance for each genre, based on the nature of that genre. Thus, if we must preserve the notion of genres, we must think of them as open classes, or multiply them. What we would say in discussing an impressionist painting must differ from what we would say in discussing a canvas by Titian and by Dubuffet. We must not treat the symphonies of Bruckner as we do the symphonies of Haydn and Beethoven. In listening to Bruckner, we need to develop an expansiveness of conception and leisureliness of procedure not necessary for Haydn. As a result of these conflicts, we have changed our preconceptions as to what constitutes the proper subject matter, technique and even media for painting or what constitutes the proper subject matter and form for poetry.

But to return to the case of tragedy, is Willy Loman a tragic figure? Supposing that we succeed in spelling out several sets of criteria for tragedy, how do we answer the question? We do the following: first we must closely observe and fully respond to the play in question; then proceed to consult our knowledge and experience of other tragedies, taking care that we understand their individual natures clearly; and last and most important of all, we must see whether our response to Willy Loman is in any way like our reaction to Oedipus, Medea, Othello, Brittanicus, etc. Thus our previous knowledge of the genre must influence what we think and how we react and even what features we think are relevant and ought to be mentioned in a critical discussion.

The discussion so far has assumed that genres, though ill-defined, changing and open, nevertheless exist. But we have said all along that works of art are unique. If the principles of tragedy prevent the *Death of a Salesman* from being a good tragedy, then so much the worse for the principles of tragedy: rather we must decide the worth of the plays on other grounds. What other grounds are there? There is an avenue of approach that we may take. To say that works of art are unique must mean, for one thing, that each individual work of art must yield its own sort of worth, based on its own nature. Since works of art are autonomous, they must be capable of an independent existence and of establishing their own worth. Whatever we say about a work of art then must be grounded on the nature of that particular work of art. For any object x, the inquiry seems to come in two stages. First we ask whether it is a good poem, whether it is a good tragedy, whether it is a good concerto or not. (These are questions about the particular object.) We may succeed, moreover, in answering these questions right away. But even if we cannot answer the question, as in the case of the *Death of a Salesman,* we can still try to decide whether it is satisfactory and significant as an aesthetic object. But sometimes we encounter a further difficulty, and questions of the following kind arise: is play x really actable? Is a canvas by Jackson Pollock really a painting? Do the sound-objects dreamt up by John Cage count as music compositions? The last two questions involve a most difficult decision as to what is the difference between a painting and mere paint dribbles; what distinguishes a sequence of musical sounds from mere noise or poetry from mere verse. These are questions partly of expertise, and for this reason they depend on knowledge and experience; but the question of what constitutes a work of art in a more general sense has also been invoked. The logic of the case is something like the following: the relevance of reasons to support an aesthetic judgment depends on the nature of the individual object of art; but sometimes the question about the definition of art in general enters the inquiry, and no blanket answer about relevance can be given except by considering particular cases (and only when necessary in the light of the general theory of art).

The foregoing conclusions mean that we cannot blindly rely on any idea of genre or category. In crucial cases the idea of a genre fails us. Many aesthetic considerations are not condition-governed because of the very uniqueness of works of art. They should be considered as individuals. Reasons, then, that are good in one case are not applicable in another. But it is also a fact that we exchange reasons in aesthetic discourse, and there are genuine arguments that lead to satisfactory conclusions in art criticism. Most of these arguments, by the very nature of art, must refer to specific features of the particular work of art. But such reasons are not universalizable. But can any consideration offered as a reason which is not universalizable function as a reason? If so, how does it manage to explain and illuminate? The following questions remain to be discussed. (1) Are there non-universalizable, unique reasons — that is, explanations that apply to one case only? (2) Do we need to revise our account of reasons? (3) Or must we withdraw the hope of argumentation, demonstration and reason-giving in aesthetic discourse?

IV

One is tempted to say that reasons are always universalizable; that is what makes them reasons. But when applied to works of art — which are unique and autonomous — they do not need to be universalizable. Thus, certain considerations (referring to the features of a work of art) may relevantly count toward an evaluation in one case. But the same features, despite their presence in another work of art, may not be relevantly applicable to another case because of their conjunction with other features of the second work which changes their nature and makes the whole object distinct. The foregoing was the account of reason-giving developed in the preceding chapter. This logical schema applies to arguments trying to show how a work of art happens to have certain aesthetic properties (e.g., that it is tense, tragic, harmonious, dramatic) as well as to arguments establishing that a painting is good or that a tragedy is a great work of art. But this schema must, at this point, be revised; for according to it aesthetic reasons are condition-governed, though by defeasible reasons. Though many, perhaps most, aesthetic arguments are condition-governed, in the crucial cases they are not so at all. The crux of this argument hinges on the uniqueness that works of art are said to have. If this is true, then we must cherish them for what they are in themselves; and their merits are *their own*.

To make the issue clearer, we may contrast aesthetic judgments with ethical judgments. When we speak of the morally good man or the morally good action, we expect whatever criteria that is

operative to apply to other cases that are relevantly similar. If x
is the correct thing to do, then the reasons that make it so, if
present in y (no other overriding considerations being present)
would make y correct. (The overriding considerations too, may
be formulated to apply to similar cases.) The moral thing to do,
whatever it is, is just that which we would will all men to do
in like circumstances. The action must be, to use a Kantian
locution, universalizable. This is the moral point of view. But
this example shows how different moral judgments are from
aesthetic judgments, for we do not want all works of art to be
alike. Nor do we wish them to please in identical ways or to
function alike. The function of morality, on the other hand,
is to bring to order and rationality disparate human motives and
responses, to render them more alike in their relation to each
other. If the difference between the two forms of logic consists in
the fact that works of art are unique, then it must be pointed out
that according to some philosophers, human beings are unique
also. Are works of art, therefore, unique in a different way?

V

We may discover what is meant by the uniqueness of a work of
art by looking at how critics utilize the notion. They do it in
several ways. A critic might say that a work of art was unique
at a certain junction of his discussion, usually toward the end,
when, along with a strong admiration and approbation, he feels
that little or nothing more could be said, especially of a comparative nature, about the work that he is discussing. He might
say that is inimitable or, simply, that it is just what it is. So a
critic may state, for example, *"The Music Party* has Watteau's
special magic, and it is because . . . he could not touch a crayon
to paper, nor a brush — even a dirty brush — to canvas, without
creating a fragment of unique and mysterious quality, that I have
chosen to discuss it here."[21] Stated simply, a work of art is
unique because no other work is like it. Taken at face value,
this is obviously not true, since there are many works of art
that resemble each other: the endless quantities of Renaissance
sonnets, Baroque madonnas swathed in clouds, the Haydnesque
and Mozartean minuets, the innumerable, almost indistinguish-
able works by the abstract expressionists. If these are resemblances
and not identities, there are works that are more closely identified: e.g., the many copies of the same print; many copies of El

Greco's "St. Martin and the beggar", even by his own hand; many performances of Mozart's operas (by the same artists); or the many renditions of Beethoven's piano sonatas. The mode of resemblances involved in each of these instances is different. But to take the case closest to complete identity, a person saying that a Mozart opera (say *Idomeneo*) is unique, means that any other opera by Mozart, e.g., *Don Giovanni* and the *Nozze di Figaro,* is different from it, and any opera by any other composer is different from the *Idomeneo* though the two may belong to the same genre. The *Idomeneo* observes many of the conventions of the 18th-century *opera seria*: the type of protagonists, the form of the arias, their arrangements within the scenes, the number of persons on the stage at any one time, their order of entrance and exit, etc. But *Idomeneo* is unique because the musical features it brings together form an organic whole which is different from that of any other opera. The complex formed is different from any other in being just that actual complex. There will be similarities among a number of *opere serie,* of course, but there will always be some interesting differences to distinguish one from the other.

This is the simple view of the uniqueness of works of art, but a number of separate points are combined in it. The notion of uniqueness is a claim based on the material nature of a work of art. Any work of art, despite its resemblance to another, would be composed of sufficiently distinguishable phenomena to make the two different — e.g., two landscapes by one artist of the same location, but captured at different times of the day (Monet). It would follow, then, that depending on the kind of material used, there would be different kinds of uniqueness. Each of the arts utilizes a different combination of senses. Further, the uniqueness that pertains to highly sensuous materials would differ from that of something relatively nonsensuous like language. In the arts, such as music and drama, the individual uniqueness possessed by a number of actual performances of a work must differ from the uniqueness among the scores or scripts of different works. Which uniqueness one would privilege — that depends on one's ontology of art. In the sense explained, any object is unique — since one can always specify the temporal-spacial location to individualize an entity. Any discrete work of art, being composed of distinct pieces of matter (or segment of reality), *must* be necessarily unique in this sense. Ontologically speaking, the uniqueness claim is trivial, since it is true of anything in the world which is discernible. The idea of uniqueness is also evaluatively neutral. Something which is unique may be, at the same time, uninteresting; the uniqueness itself is not a merit. But the claim may still make a difference, since we can always treat works of art scientifically, morally, historically rather than aesthetically. There are many ways of treating things, and this realization shows that the claim for uniqueness can become nondescriptive; perhaps it tells us how we ought to deal with works of art. Or perhaps it says something about the intention of works of art (though not necessarily the intention of the artists). The question that we would eventually like to answer is what it is like to treat things aesthetically. This simple view of uniqueness then lays its emphasis on the concrete particularity of works of art. But it can account for the uniqueness of works of art that are called abstract. Looking at a painting by Mondrian or a very plain Persian filigree, we are charmed by the abstract pattern; but in the actual work, the pattern is presented to us concretely in its full specificity. A critic who discusses an abstract painting finds what is aesthetically worthwhile in the actual quality of lines, the texture of the surface and the peculiar suitability of these to the expression. What is abstract is nevertheless given a concrete manifestation, for the surface texture of the painting is an essential part of the object. In literature, for example, the universal aspects of character and events (the plot) pointed out by literary critics are repeatable. But their manifestation in a literary work is concrete; for we say that the plot and characters of a story or a play are inseparable from their expression. In saying that a work is abstract, we mean that the artist has pared down the details, emphasized the abstract pattern, but presented just the parts he has, in their concreteness. The intuitionist and idealist theories of art (e.g., those of Croce, Collingwood) depend on this last point — that in the cognition of art, we exercise a mode of knowing (a way of cognizing or communicating) which is sensuously concrete, particular, immediate and nonabstract. Some of them have further insisted that this mode of cognition can be exercised on anything in the world, but we do not bother to do so for reasons of inattention, preoccupation with utility, etc.

The relationship of the notion of uniqueness to the different kinds of materials that constitute the substance of works of art should be developed in more detail. The question of particularity is relatively easily handled in the visual and musical arts. We emphasize the sensuous concreteness of the object. We can see how a canvas or even two versions (i.e., canvasses) of the same work by the artist himself can be claimed to be each a particularity. We try to judge them on their independent merits, not on their sameness. (Notice the prescriptive aspect of this thesis.) There may be subtle differences between the two; and one may be better than the other, or both may be good, though in different ways, or their merits may be undecidable. If we could not see any difference (if that were possible) we would say that they were the same (but not, therefore, that they were not unique). Rather we would take each as equally authentic, for we are interested not in the type but the concrete manifestation of the work. This is nicely seen in the study of prints. Prints and etchings are *made* for reproductions. This makes for some important differences in the way we evaluate prints from easel paintings; but not as regards their uniqueness. Many copies of prints even in the same edition show subtle differences. It is the sign of a true connoisseur or a good critic that he can discover these differences and see whether they make an aesthetic difference or not. Some of these differences (perhaps an accident of the printing process) may make a copy less expressive, thus marring it. On the other hand, two versions of a woodcut with different arrangements of colors may be equally effective. Whatever the case, each copy of a print must be judged on its own merits. If the copies are all miraculously alike, then they are all on a par as regards their value. And we would say that each one is an "original." We cannot reproduce paintings quite so effectively or perfectly as we can prints. But if two or more copies of a work come down to us (especially from the master's hand) we should judge them all (identical or not) on their individual merits. In principle, it is possible for a copy to be better than the original or to display merits vastly different from the original — as in the examples of Rubens' copies of Titians, done at the request of Philip IV. In the latter case, why not say that they are different works?

But it is more difficult to explain the particularity of literary works on the basis of their sensuous concreteness. Except in poetry, where the quality of sound itself is made prominent, there seems to be nothing particularly concrete or sensuous in literary works as far as their material substance (the language) goes. Almost anything other than proper names in the following passage from a novel by Conrad seems abstract.

> In the face of a man's desire a girl is excusable if she thinks
> herself priceless. I mean a girl of our civilization which has
> established a dithyrambic phraseology for the expressing of love.

A man in love will accept any convention exalting the object of his passion and in this indirect way his passion itself. In what way the captain of the *Ferndale* gave proof of lover-like lavishness I could not guess very well. But I was glad she was appreciative. It is lucky that small things please women. And it is not silly of them to be thus pleased. It is in small things that the deepest loyalty, that which they need most, the loyalty of the passing moment, is best expressed.22

How is the medium of the novel used aesthetically? One may emphasize the quality of sound in the language and press the visual and aural images for all they are worth. But this is as sensuous as language can get. In general, the question is not answered on the basis of the sensuous qualities of the medium nor on the grounds that the matter is inseparable from the work of art. For, after all, many important works of literature have been successfully translated. Their uniqueness consists first in the actual arrangement of thought, images, events; second in the comment and view points that merge from their arrangement, and most of all, in the quality of mind that becomes apparent. (We do not pay much attention to the various copies or edition of texts except for historical reasons. If the texts themselves show differences, then we settle the issue, first by trying to discover which the author intended, and if this is impossible, to determine which version is the most effective — which we assume is what the author would have intended to begin with.) Sometimes the turns of thought, the sorts of images and concepts that predominate are called the style of the writer. If this is what style is, it is independent of the physical language itself. Style then is the man. However, we often mean by the style, the manner in which the author manipulates his language, especially its rhythms and quality of sound. To the extent that these two senses of style are inseparable, the uniqueness consists also in the sensuous qualities of the language. But it is also more. The idea of style (or styles) presupposes a similarity among works of art — for we speak of the style of a period, the style of an artist, though at the same time, it maintains its hold on the disparateness of works of art. Only objects that are really different can display the similarity of style.

The doctrine of uniqueness is a maxim to the effect that you must treat works of art as if they had intrinsic merits of their own; that their concrete particular embodiment must generate their own individual values. The doctrine at least has the heuristic value of pointing out the detrimental effect of over-emphasizing the scripts of plays and the scores of musical compositions. Plays and music acquire their reality in their full physical reenactment; and while we need to examine the ways in which they depart from the directions given in the text or the score, there will obviously be ways in which alternative embodiments will be allowed by the directions. The texts of plays and scores of musical compositions may be specific in their notations, but they are never concrete and particular. There may be equally effective interpretations of *Hamlet* that are very different; very different phrasings of the same melodies, all of them consistent with the score or the text. Even a performance of *Hamlet* that departed widely from the text may be an effective work of art; though perhaps no longer Shakespeare's *Hamlet,* beyond a certain point. Each enactment then must be seen on its own. And the critical mind must have the perspicacity and the agility to respond to each case on its own merits, while balancing this amplitude with the expertise that comes with experience and the knowledge of tradition.

Sheer difference and particularity is not enough to account for the notion of uniqueness. Take the example of Renaissance love sonnets. If uniqueness consists in the arrangements of words and ideas alone, they are all different. But somehow, beyond the first two dozen, they all begin to seem monotonously the same. They conform to a type. Sonnets by minor poets seem routine and obvious. And we begin to wish for some spark of originality. Poets naturally (to stick with the example of the Elizabethan sonnets) sought after "something that would 'astonish' and 'amaze' "[23] — a new style and texture, new effects ("less emotional and more intellectual, less sweet and more piquant"), new subject matter, a new order of reality. At this juncture, the idea of novelty takes on an ontological cast. One can suggest (as I am inclined to) that works of art make manifest to us the extraordinary *looks* of things — especially in the paradigm cases of the tragic, the sublime and the visionary. Such works (e.g. Beethoven's last quartets, Goya's prints, the poems of Blake, Emily Dickinson, the novels of Melville) reveal to us another order of reality, and what they make manifest is something new, created *ex nihilo,* though in the sensous matter of our world. But even the matter is made to seem different, for we see them differently. This transcendent, magical aspect of art is as much a part of the essence of art as the mimetic and the beautiful. It is for this reason that we ultimately value the unique in art and find it worth our while to treat works of art as autonomous.

The idea of novelty is thus contained in the idea of uniqueness, since, if one wants to be different, striking a new effect is the most ready means available to an artist. It is the easiest way: though not the subtlest. But in the final analysis, an artist must produce the best (most significant, nearly perfect) entity he is capable of. And novelty can be achieved in this way too; by "doing more continuously or to a higher degree something that had been done before."[24] At this point, the notion of novelty has become evaluative in significance, although originally, it was evaluatively neutral. Originality, in itself, is of no particular merit except as an attention-getter. How much repetition can we take and still hold our interest focussed? There is no obvious answer; but if a work is worthless, even if it is astonishingly original, we would not pay any attention. And if the work says something which is worth paying attention to, we would not mind the repetitions. But psychologically, it is difficult to pay attention to something repetitiously monotonous. The works of strength, those works of art that are "original" and those that have attained a perfection (whether they come early or later in the history of the art) are works of genius, and they come, eventually to represent the whole genus as paradigmatic examples. "The sonnets [of Shakespeare] are the very heart of the Golden Age, the highest and purest achievement of the Golden way of writing."[25] The idea of uniqueness, thus, is a complex one, consisting of the ideas of particularity, novelty, and significance. The task of the critic is to reveal by what he says the significance of a work of art, its merits, the interest it holds for us, while keeping in the foreground its originality, its differentness as well as its particularity.

VI

What can we say now about aesthetic arguments in the light of the preceding discussion of the uniqueness of works of art?   In aesthetic arguments, we attempt to build a case for the plausibility of a certain reading, a certain viewing, a certain interpretation of various works of art. We also attempt to justify the evaluative judgments that are based on such readings and interpretations. These two processes are not always clearly separable, but in doing either of these we offer reasons of the appropriate sort that refer to a particular work of art.   I want to limit the following comments to the establishing of evaluative assessments. (1) The considerations that we offer are usually feature-reasons.   These

feature reasons we find quasi-generalizations present either ex-
universalized in a mechanical manner. Sometimes, along with
feature reasons we find quasi-generalizations, present either ex-
plicitly or implicitly. For any such generalization, however, in
principle we can find counter-examples. Any historical or psychological generalization about works of art has exceptions. And
many works of art are successful, despite their violation of rule
(and conditions) formulated by earlier critics and aestheticians.
(2) This is the situation because works of art by their nature are
unique and thus autonomous with respect to rules and standards.
The good-making points of a work of art which we proffer as
backing for our assertions, if correctly present, *will* in point of
fact show that this particular work of art is good, but it will
be true only for this case. (3) It may happen that the feature
itself, or a cluster of them, could recur in a number of works, and
in each of these cases, contribute to the virtue of that work.
But we must not expect to be able to reapply such feature-reasons
in a mechanical fashion to all other cases. (4) We expect reasons
to explain and to support. Aesthetic reasons despite their un-
repeatability do manage to support and explain. But this characteristic contradicts an important feature of thinking and understanding, for one of the clearcut ways in which we come to
understand something is by associating it with other things, seeing their similarities and categorizing them. If, however, the
very nature of the object makes it impossible that these entities
be categorized, then this schema for reason-giving cannot apply
to them. What then shall we conclude about the logic of criticism?
We can say that although aesthetic reasons do explain and support
a value judgment (and this is a fact of the case), they are not
subject to the requirement of universalizability. But then how
do they explain and support? This can be shown by carefully
examining many cases of fine, successful criticism. It can be
shown only by example, since critical discourse is concrete,
and cannot proceed by generality without grave danger. The
inapplicability of the principle of universalizability accounts for
this situation. The logic of art criticism can be described. But the
principles and standards of criticism cannot be set down. Nor
can a general account of how aesthetic reasons function in each
particular case be given, since every case is quite different from
all the others. Then how do critics work? They wrestle with the
particular object before them, trying to come to a thorough understanding of it, for there is no other way of undertaking the evalua-

tion of a unique object. Though unique, the object nevertheless belongs to a stream of other objects more or less like it. The critic therefore needs to know a great deal about the stream, be it the history of the media itself or the class of objects by the same creator. What the critic does is assess the object — his many observations (each one of them in turn re-assessable) working together to lend credence to the final assessment. The process must, of course, illuminate and explain the work of art as well as the assessment; and, in turn, we expect a clear, reasonable, appropriate account.

There are other cases in which the nature of the entity rules out the possibility of repeatable, universal reasons. A brief examination of two examples may help clarify the case of aesthetic reasons. Both historical events and individual persons are said to be unique. By this we mean that historical events do not repeat themselves, and that ultimately no person is like another. If these claims are true, then what is true of a historical event or of a person cannot be generalized and reapplied to other cases. How can we shift from event to event (as we do in our history lessons) and say that we understand them? How does knowing one person help us to understand another?

Is it true that events do not repeat themselves? Their temporal and spatial discreteness (though actual) is not enough to make events unique. At first glance there seems to be nothing in the nature of historical events to prevent their reoccurrence — at least the recurrence of an event sufficiently like another so that one can say they were the same. There are many events that have general labels attached to them, such as revolutions, wars, economic crashes; and they must have similarities in order to deserve such labels. And indeed there are similarities. But events, especially those that are historically interesting, like the Dreyfus case, the Russian revolution, the assassination of Abraham Lincoln, the Florentine Renaissance, are highly complex and this complexity accounts for their uniqueness. [26] For seen in their infinite complexity it is difficult to believe that such events would recur — especially with the identical individuals involved. But as historians we cannot simply be awed into silence by the infinite complexity of events. For discursive purposes, we greatly simplify events. We pick out the similarities that one has in common with another— relevant similar features, for example, of the American and Russian revolutions. But we also look at the dissimilarities. Historians not only make comparison; they also attempt to see the

113

differences between one event and another — they look for the uniqueness of events. What makes the French revolution different from all other previous revolutions? And by finding the differences, historians come to understand the French revolution. In other words, they *look* for the distinguishing, individualizing elements in events. This procedure distinguishes historians from anthropologists and sociologists. The latter, being scientists, look for generalizations, principles and statistical correlations. Historians describe and explain concrete events in their contexts. Their primary concern is not to form law-like historical generalizations. Ancient historians, for example, are interested in what happened in 44 B.C., Rome; what were the events leading up to the happening, and what were the consequences. There are general truths that apply to the case. But what the historians principally want to know is what makes for the distinctive features of the events of 44 B.C. The differences are, of course, due to the complex features of the antecedent events (including the intentions of men), any of which perhaps appear in other events; but as a complex whole, the event is unique. This, however, in no way makes it impossible for historians to ascertain the facts of the case, to argue pros and cons of tentative explanations and interpretations and to come to an understanding of the facts.

Human beings, too, according to some philosophers and some scientists are unique. This is not to deny that human beings belong to a species and to various subspecies, and the laws of psychology and sociology group people into fairly large categories. But on a common sense level, we believe that although human beings are alike (that is why we recognize character-traits from person to person), in the final analysis, there are rock-bottom ways in which people are unlike each other. Perhaps this is because, aside from our differing biological and temperamental inheritances, we all undergo, over a long range of time, significantly different influences. The combination is infinitely complex. For scientific, legal or social purposes we must treat each other as falling into definite (and conventional) categories; but to understand a person, we must come to grips with his fundamental uniquenesses. To say, then, that human beings are unique, might be interpreted in a regulative fashion to mean that we should regard all human beings as unique (in some relevantly specified respects). (It is not merely the descriptive assertion that human beings are complex and fundamentally different.) We believe that to love and understand a person, we must see him just as he is: complex, ever-changing, unique. We may raise this maxim itself to the status of a moral philosophy (it has been done), but the more common view is to contrast the ethical view to it. To treat a person morally is to treat him as you would any other person (the sort of treatment being further specified). Or to say "all moral valuations are of type-U." One might object that if all human beings were utterly complex, unique, and contingent (because each feature is inextricably contingent on another), then we can never come to understand anyone at all. But this view would be open to question. If true, it only *means* that the task of understanding another human being is never done. And in a sense, do we ever *really* understand a person? It would be presumptuous to say so. Or the subject must be remarkably simple. But in the final analysis, do we not all find that our best friends sometime surprise us by revealing new and unsuspected facets of their character? Yet for all practical purposes our interim understandings will do: we find out enough about others to allow us to relate and interact as persons with them. And that is sufficient knowledge for our purposes.

I do not claim that the comprehension of a work of art is like the comprehension of historical events or of individual persons. That would be oversimple. But we can wonder how we can ever come to understand and appreciate works of art that are unique without the use of universal standards. Then I suggest that there are other examples of unique entities with which our understanding comes to grips. And we do not say that they are utterly incomprehensible.

VII

I now summarize. (1) We usually say that reasons function as reasons by virtue of the fact that they also apply to other relevant cases. A reason cannot be a reason if it applies only to one case. (2) But in dealing with entities that are unique in some essential manner, the requirement of reasons applying to other relevant cases cannot always be fulfilled. Do such reasons still deserve the name of "reasons"? (3) The answer hinges partly on the sort of uniqueness claimed, but we can see from an examination of aesthetic arguments that reasons that cannot be universalized can still explain and support a judgment. In this sense, they are reasons, though unlike moral reasons and causal reasons that are universalizable.

7 | CRITICISM AND TASTE

We expect the way in which a connoisseur sees and analyzes an object of art to influence the interest and enjoyment he takes in it and his evaluative judgment of it. The task ought to be all of one piece. Quite rightly, then, we expect the critic, when he makes an evaluative judgment, to offer some kind of consideration in support of such evaluation. And if his judgment differs from that of another critic, we expect to find that their comprehension of the work differs. But on closely studying the various cases of disagreement, we discover that no clear pattern of agreement and disagreement emerges. People agree in their interest and liking, disagree in their analysis and description and may or may not agree in their evaluative dicta. But there is a logic in aesthetic discourse, for considerations offered in support of an evaluative judgment can be either relevant or irrelevant. In this chapter, the whole problem of the adjudication of these differences and how they arise will be examined. In order to simplify the task of scrutinizing the disagreement among critics, the variety of disagreements are summarized in the following table:

	Analysis	*Judgments*	*Attitudes*
a	A	A	A
b	A	A	D
c	A	D	A
d	A	D	D
	D	A	A
	D	A	D
	D	D	A
	D	D	D

The table is constructed on the analogue of a truth table: letter A represents agreement, D represents disagreement. By attitude we mean the critic's tastes, and it includes his way of looking at a work of art, if he has a special slant, as well as his liking or disliking of it. The designations *a, b, c,* and *d* refer to situations that I shall want to discuss in detail.

116

I

Special cases of disagreement are those in which the critics cannot even agree as to how the work of art is to be viewed. They present strikingly different analysis, and their descriptions may seem to refer to two different events or objects (the last four rows of the table).

Where two different objects (in some sense) seem to be in question, it does not surprise us that the critics should be in disagreement. From such a disagreement, the claim of the relativity of taste does not follow. It has, however, frequently been claimed that no two persons ever see the same painting, hear the same music. It is not uncommon to hear that "If x has disagreements with y on musical matters, he is entitled to his opinion. We may not agree with him, but no music sounds the same to any two people, so that we can only shrug our shoulder if x's taste does not coincide with y's."[1] If no music sounds the same to two persons, what then is the music? Where is it? How do we discover that it does not sound the same to two people? The differences need to be brought out into the open so that we may understand their nature. There are various techniques for doing so. We usually ask the critics to describe the work and their reaction to it. We may discover some physical and physiological factors in the observation to explain the differences in their analyses. There may be a faulty comprehension of the work of art. For example, a simple mistake about the genre and one which may be rectified. The two critics may be working from different contexts. What a Roman Catholic critic says, if he lets his religion influence his talk, would differ from a Marxist's criticism. They may both say wonderful and very illuminating things about a work of art, which, moreover, may be true. But because they look at the work with "different eyes," we do not expect their reports to agree. The difference may turn out to be a clear case of prejudice. In such a case, the critic comes to the work of art with a presupposition. We can see how this presupposition influences the analysis and we can also show how the presupposition has been imported into the case. It would then be irrelevant. The presupposition must also be avoidable. Unavoidable presuppositions are not "prejudices." Unless we can discover that the presupposition is there and that it is irrelevant, we could not claim that it is a "prejudice." Even without these large and heavy-handed presuppositions looming in the background, people have frequently

117

disagreed on the analysis of a work of art. Ambiguity in a work of art — for example, the enigma of Hamlet's motivation or the Gioconda's smile — may give rise to the disagreement, although the ambiguous quality of some works of art — *Moby Dick, Don Giovanni,* the novels of Kafka or the late quartets of Beethoven — makes them all the more fascinating.

II

We go on to the cases in which the critics agree. (1) (*a*) in the preceding table is a case of complete unanimity, and nothing more needs to be said about it, except that it is a rare state of affairs. (2) Critics may agree in analysis and attitude but disagree in their evaluation of the work of art (as in *c*). This seems to be a case of evaluative disagreement, for differing evaluations are "supported" by similar analyses and tastes. Is such a case possible? (Two critics may analyse *Moll Flanders* pretty much alike, both enjoy reading it but rank it differently.)[2]   Where two persons disagree in their judgments, we would expect them at least to show a difference in their comprehension of the work of art, as suggested earlier. Something must make the difference; yet if the analyses of the work are also sufficiently alike, then we must look for the differences in their tastes. The case we have before us is a puzzler because the critics agree in analysis and attitude, yet they evaluate the work differently. It is logically odd. How could two persons both enjoy a work of art and comprehend it in the same way and disagree about its merits? When it happens what shall we say? We had better remind ourselves that analyzing and evaluating are not such disparate activities. We rightly expect a consistency of some sort. If we say of a work, accurately or not, that it is not very coherent and that the levels of allegory do not fuse into a unified symbol, we have described it and we have come to an understanding of it. At the same time we have down-graded it.

Evaluative judgments are expected to be related to the analysis of a work of art, for the working presupposition of all criticism and appreciation is that a judgment must be an enlightened one, one that can be backed up by relevant reasons. That we expect reasons to follow shows that we presuppose a connection. Of course this expectation may be ill-founded, and all criticism may be an illusion. In the language of criticism, however, there is a logical difference in saying "x is good" and "I like x" and part

118

of the job of criticism is to indicate why certain works are worth studying and what makes them worthwhile.

3) Of the two remaining cases, (d) first. We would suspect right away that the critic' attitudes have conditioned their evaluation (and that at least one of them is wrong). For otherwise, we would be faced with the oddity that the first critic says the work is good, the second critic that it is not; and both give the same reasons (and they must, since their comprehension of the work is the same, as in c). We would then try to explain the difference in evaluation by pointing out the difference in attitude. There are examples for this from nonaesthetic cases. A judge in a beauty contest may not vote for a red-headed contestant, as did all the other judges, because he did not like redheads for personal reason. He may know what the rules are and be able to apply them correctly. He may also admit that the red-headed contestant qualifies in all other respects and still refuse to vote for her. Hatred of the Chinese may make a gourmet deride Cantonese cuisine, and an anti-German person may dislike the operas of Wagner.

4) Logically, (b) and (d) are alike in that in both there is a difference in taste and a similarity in comprehension. They differ only in that in the case of (b) there is an agreement in evaluation. This frequently happens and it is not surprising. It is natural that even people who make similar cognitive judgments should have dissimilar tastes. Bernard Berenson, who we know did not care much for the modern movements in art, could, nevertheless, discuss and judge Matisse and Picasso in ways that Clive Bell need not have taken any great exception to.[3] A person may say, for example, that in painting, his taste inclines toward the modernists. He does not suggest in so saying that he does not understand the others or that his evaluation would always coincide with his preferences. All he means is that his liking leans that way and that he may be more sensitive to the nuances that he discovers in an expressionist painting. But it is just these cases [(b) and (d)] that explain what it means to say that tastes differ.

"So there are these differences in taste!" What conclusion do we imply in pointing this out? Philip II did not like El Greco. (Many people do not.) José de Sigüenza, one of Philip's agents wrote that the *Theban Legion,* "commissioned for an alter in the church of the Escorial . . . did not please his Majesty — it is not much — for it pleases few, although they say it is a great art, and that its author knows a lot, and there are excellent things

119

to be seen by his hand. In this there are many opinions and tastes."[4] Sigüenza is not merely stating this as a biographical fact, though at this late date, it is most interesting. What he does is to put King Philip's taste above criticism. It is granted that this work, according to some, has merit (is "great art") but it is also suggested that it makes no difference to the king's pleasure. Nor does he see that it is great art. (Would it make a difference to his enjoyment if he did?) Two incompatible claims are being made at the same time. One claim is that enjoyment and value judgment are independent of each other, for the quotation says that many say it is a great art though few take pleasure in it. The second claim (which goes counter to the first) is that value judgments are based on the taste of the critic, and taste is beyond further adjudication, ("There are excellent things to be seen . . . in this there are many opinions and tastes.") Since evaluative judgments are based on taste, which is relative and groundless, one cannot say it is incorrect. The whole question of the validity of value judgments must not arise. The intention is that of disqualifying all evaluative judgments in art criticism. It is a matter of taste. If you like it, it is good for you, and that is what "good" really amounts to.

III

If there is this rock-bottom disagreement in the enjoyment and pleasures of persons, are we justified in saying, as we sometimes do, that some tastes are more cultivated than others or that someone's taste has been improved? Are there competent judges of these things? (Critics often make embarrassing mistakes in judgment.) It is not true that persons who have adequately experienced a wide variety of works of art invariably choose the best. When a person claims that all taste is relative and that all value judgments are subjective, he implies that no taste is more cultivated than another or better than another. After all, there is no standard of taste. It would follow, therefore, that if there were a standard of taste, it would presuppose a standard of good and bad art, which must consist of an objective account of what worthiness and excellence are in art. Or lacking that, at least a relatively universal inventory of what are indisputably good works of art.

I do not propose to develop an account of the nature of art here. But at this juncture, we can admit that in oriental as well as in occidental art there is a high degree of agreement as to what are the masterpieces. To this class of objects, there are two ways of responding. We can emphasize the way in which we like them and find them entertaining and pleasing. Or we can emphasize what we find worth noticing and understanding in them, and how what we notice is rewarding. The varieties of pleasure and enjoyment that we can garner are many (e.g., the difference between the pleasures of a Chinese landscape and those of a late Picasso). But there is also a great variety among the merits of a work of art (e.g., the rewards from Claude Lorraine are different from those of a Van Gogh). It is then easy to see how what is worthwhile and what is pleasant may be independent of each other. There are some works of art whose reward *consists* in the pleasure that we receive from them on an initial encounter (e.g., some Japanese woodcuts, the paintings of Renoir); but there are many others that are worthy of study though not pleasant at all (Grünewald, Kandinsky, much Rembrandt). Both types are equally *art*. Many things are pleasure-yielding — and among them, fortunately, we find works of art. But any work of art, needless to say, can be treated, not as art but as something that is principally pleasant and entertaining or even as an object of utility. We need to guard against confusing objects that are primarily pleasant with works of art. Logically, that someone should like an object is neither the necessary nor the sufficient condition for its being a work of art. Of course, it would be wrong to neglect the fact that many works of art are pleasant. It is probably one of the first qualities that causally provoke our interest. Moreover, pleasant things are easier to study, collect and contemplate. So we tend to concentrate our attention on works of art that we like very much. But it is easy to confuse or identify the idea of art and that of pleasure. Our concept of a work of art, however, has also become blurred because we tend to view the contents of museums solely as collections of *good* works of art and not of objects that we (or our ancestors) have found pleasing. Thus, in studying the history of any of the arts, we emphasize the disparity in aesthetic taste that we think is revealed there. This, I believe, is a mistake. The famous national collections of art are as much collections of things that were loved (with a sentimental-ancestral "value" to them) as they are collections of great works of art. Things that people enjoy change. But we also say time reveals what the great masterpieces are. Yet it is surprising how often we have recognized the great works of art from the start. A reading of the history of collecting shows how right many collectors have been, in spite of some embarrassing mistakes (mid-nineteenth-century French salon art, the late nineteenth-century craze for Daubigny and the Barbizon school, or the Japanese disdain for their traditional woodcuts). The list of the paintings that connoisseurs from all over Europe vied to purchase from the collection of Charles I, put up for sale in Amsterdam by the Puritan Parliament, rings with familiar names. If Philip II made a mistake in El Greco, then his favorite painters were Titian and Bosch. The collection of Philip IV, especially of the works of painters that he directly patronized (Velásquez, Rubens, Van Dyck), which now fills the Museum of the Prado is most impressive.[5] We do not ask for infallibility, only for more hits than misses. One suspects, further, that our knowledge of the history of taste is faulty. A recent music lover, after an extensive survey of musical criticism in London from 1800 to 1914, remarks that he was "fascinated to see not only how fundamentally right most of the critics were, in spite of prejudiced mistakes due to the taste of the day, but also how that taste changed through the years."[6] When we say or imply that we like something, we do not mean thereby that it is a work of art.

Further, we must not always blame the critics when they disagree. Some works of art demand a very special taste — and this means that if we wish to understand and appreciate them, we must acquire that taste. Unless we have a highly developed capacity for dispassionate contemplation, we will not be able to study things that we dislike with impartiality. In many works of art, the range of experience, the language, the palette, the tonalities that an artist has emphasized are, to say the least, eccentric. I take the following extreme example from a notice circulated by a book club.

> DOWN THERE (Là Bas). *By J. K. Huysmans.* This infamous nineteenth-century novel by an inferior disciple of Edmond de Goncourt, Zola, and Flaubert is for special taste. Blasphemous and decadent, it dwells on a weird world of sexual abnormality, erotic mysticism, incubism, succubism, and bestiality.[7]

Special taste are acquired by effort; we do not expect them to be present, unless they have been cultivated. And their absence accounts for the disparity in the stock values placed on certain works through the ages. These works have been seen only through the spectrum of taste. Hence their valuation. Their intrinsic merit

122

is quite another thing. For that, we must scrutinize the objects themselves, and not through special spectacles.

Whenever persons differ in taste, it is perfectly natural to suspect a difference in sensitivity, experience and in knowledge. These factors can make a difference in our reactions. But admitting this possibility takes away a great deal of the charm from the doctrine of the relativity of taste. For the admission seems to suggest that without these differences, our responses in enjoyment may be more alike. Our system of aesthetic education takes into account this recognition and gives the lie to relativism. If we care about works of art, we train ourselves to overcome the personal, idiosyncratic ways of responding to them and the limitations that we inherit from our social environment. There are ways to "improve" our tastes. It is possible to achieve improvement, and there is nothing mysterious about the process.

We can now be explicit about the qualification of a person of taste. He is one who can (has trained himself to) moderate his "taste responses" with the knowledge that he has of works of art. He can discriminate and see what is worthwhile; and knowing what is good, likes it. A person of taste in this strict sense is different from a person who has taste because he is sensitive to the aesthetic qualities of things. Though remarks like "this is dynamic" or "the characters are sensitively delineated" are relevant to an evaluative judgment, the aesthetic properties themselves are still neutral. A painting may be dynamically organized and not be a good painting. The exercise of taste-sensitivity thus precedes, and is not identical with, the exercise of taste in this stricter, more complex sense.

Persons of taste are fewer in number than people who know a great deal about works of art. Art historians, museum directors and musicologists know much about the objects they study, but they do not necessarily like what they know to be worthwhile. (A museum director could overestimate the worth of a certain painter. And in principle, he might even realize this. He could say "Yes, I know that I overestimate the values of these works, but I like them very much because I have been working with them for a long time." Then, knowing this to be the case, if he were conscientious and scrupulous, he would hesitate before deciding to purchase works by that painter.) Likewise, a person may take great pleasure in what he *knows* to be not so admirable — enjoying show tunes, calendar art, detective fiction, Puccini's operas. That one should not like what he knows to be admirable and vice versa is not unfamiliar (though perhaps illogical). The case is strictly parallel to the incontinent man as described by Aristotle.[8] The morally incontinent man knows what it is to be virtuous and knows what he ought to do but fails to make his actions conform to his knowledge of what is good and what he expects of himself. He may know that he ought to avoid causing pain, he may lament the fact that he does so; but nevertheless he cannot prevent himself from doing so. He is weak-willed perhaps. The case could be made worse: he may derive an indirect and peculiar pleasure from being cruel. For the same reason, a person may be fallible in choosing works of art. Though his expertise may be profound, in his liking he may be influenced by factors other than the merits of the work under consideration. He may be swayed by a love of the subject matter, the style of a period, or the fashion of his times. But it is possible to be tasteful. It is possible because one can say which items are good and which are bad. To be a person of taste is to let one's knowledge and preference coincide and put oneself insofar as possible above the dictates of predilection or fashion. In this context, a tasteless person is one whose preferences are purely capricious or one who prefers the bad, knowing the better. In the strict sense, a deep knowledge of art is a necessary condition for the exercise of taste. It is possible for a person to know nothing or relatively little about art and yet manage to have all the correct preferences, namely those of someone who knows a great deal. Though ordinary English allows such a person to be called a "person of taste" (we may even say he has innate taste), he is not a person of taste in a more rigorous sense.

Although we would all like to be persons of taste, we do not worry much if we are not (nor do we make much effort to correct the bad tastes of our friends), because we do not find aesthetic correctness as important as moral rectitude. To some extent we are the same with regard to food preferences. However, we draw some lines. We do not say that cannibalism is a matter of taste; nor do we say the same of a badly balanced diet. Here the concern for human welfare enters in, and as for our diets, there is not a complete relativity. We would not wish a person to live on a bad diet or one which would cause him harm and pain. Our choice of wines (though fine discriminations are made) is still a "matter of taste." If we feel strongly that people are better off for comprehending works of art and being sensitive to their many values and that societies in which such comprehension and sensitivity abound are better places to live in, then we may go so far as to say — as has been said in some societies in the past — that people should develop their tastes.

IV

There seems to be a number of distinct ideas of what taste is.

1) Taste is the exercise of sensitivity. Persons who have developed a capacity to detect various aesthetic properties are tasteful.

2) Taste is also a matter of brute liking — something which is thought to be free-floating. One usually thinks of gustatory taste in this connection.

3) The strictest use of the term is that in which a person likes and enjoys works of art (or anything else) that are known, by the subject himself, to be good. An aesthetic nihilist would deny this sense and he would imply that the very goodness of a work of art is a matter of brute liking and one's liking can legitimately alight on anything one wishes (as in sense 2 above).

4) The dominant use of the word taste, however, differs from those previously cited. Usually, the term tasteful applies to preferences that are chic, smart and *a la mode*. This is a purely social sense; and naturally what is *a la mode* would change with the mode. What is proper according to the mode is purely contextual and relative. Edwardian taste (chic) in interior decoration (notice who their fashionable painters were — Whistler, Sargeant, Beardsley) is different from the taste of the mid-1930's; and it is open to question whether they are commensurate, except from a completely different, third view point; namely that of architecture as an art. But the idea of taste as allied with fashion indicates that perhaps the idea of taste is trivial and unimportant in art criticism, except in sense (1).[9] For why *must* we enjoy, or take pleasure in works of art? It is true that many works of art are pleasant, and they ought to be enjoyed. But they must be enjoyed because they are pleasant and enjoy*able* — not because they are works of art. At the same time one must keep in mind that, in any ordinary sense, *many* works of art are neither pleasant nor enjoyable. What is more, there are works of art that were created for the sake of the antiaesthetic or for the sake of the ugly. We say of such creations, uncomfortably, that "they are experiences." It would be wrong to *like* them, to take pleasure in them or to enjoy them. We submit ourselves to the

125

compelling power of such works; we study them, scrutinize them for what we can get out of them; but if we say we enjoy them, or like them, we are beginning to lose sight of our sense of values.

5) There is also taste in etiquette and social conduct. We should notice that it is possible to describe a misbehavior as a case of bad taste because the social offense is not a major one. If the misdemeanor involves the loss of life or endangers the very possibility of social existence, we would call it by a more serious name. A person who takes the possibility of eternal damnation seriously would never say that a lapse in the observation of religious ritual was a case of bad taste. It takes a good bit of detachment to be "aesthetic" about impious or immoral deeds.

What counts as a case of social bad taste, obviously differs from society to society. It depends on the details of the cultural pattern of the society and its style of life. Perhaps like the range of things that we can take pleasure in, the variations in the way (to take an example) our sexual sensibility may be organized is legion. There are noticeable differences in the style of life in Sparta and in Neronian Rome. But it becomes clear then that the organization of the crucial aspects of our social behavior does not depend on taste but on more fundamental conditions, historical, geographical and economic. Further, we can evaluate societies on moral grounds. It would be regrettable if we acquiesced in the Roman pattern of conduct or welcomed the narrow, authoritarian puritanism of Sparta. There are more moderate, better ways of living.

It is worth pointing out, too, that when we say of a society that it is guided purely by considerations of taste — as is frequently said of eighteenth-century French society or of the aristocratic society of tenth-century Japan[10] — such statements suggest that perhaps much that we value more — the sense of truth and honesty, the sense of humanity and moral sensibility — had to be suppressed in order for the rule of taste to be possible. We are thus making an oblique moral judgment.

If we call an immoral deed an act in bad taste, we are making a bad joke. The issues are too serious for jest.

III | THE MEANING OF ART

8 ⎸ TOWARDS A DEFINITION OF "ART"

There are many dogmas in the philosophy of art. But as a conclusion to this study of criticism, can we say something briefly which would show why works of art are worth bothering about? This asks for a definition of art. Such a description of the nature of a work of art requires the answer to come in two steps. First, it is necessary to state what the essence of a work of art is and then to describe the influence on human agents of their commerce with works of art, since this human effect is a vital part of the phenomenon of art.

I

Can the idea of a work of art, in the most general sense, be stated? The first answer that one is tempted to give is a negative one. If we take seriously the view that works of art are unique and autonomous, then these very characteristics would prevent any two works of art from having any essential properties in common and the task of definition is made impossible.

How far can this position be held? The view (or a version of it) is worth working out in detail to see what it amounts to .[1] We experience concrete, particular works of art. Works of art exist, but there is no such thing as Art. The actual manifestation is what is important: not the general formula, recipe, score, script, etc. Nor any reproductions. If we wish to speak about art in a more general way, it may be fruitful to discuss the potentiality, range and limits of the substance out of which it is created. But a discussion of the idea of Art, independent of all particularity, is entirely meaningless. The stuff out of which artists create their objects differs as widely as do the media available. We stipulate of each of these media as form that it must use its ingredients in a characteristic and resourceful manner. We expect the novel to present something that it alone (in its form as well as its medium) can mediate, and we expect a poem to say something that cannot be said in prose. If one gave a definition of the literary arts, the definition would probably not cover the drama. A definition of the art of literature would probably not be adequate to the idea of architecture, since the function and the media of literature differ greatly from those of architecture. We may progressively go through a careful description of the nature of sculpture and how it functions; we may do the same for architecture, showing what ingredients from nature it utilizes for unique and characteristic expression, etc. Having done so, we would end up with as many definitions as there are media (however we count them), but we would not have reached a general definition of art itself, except one arrived at by a process of elimination: a definition composed of a series of relatively empty notions which might be true of all of the media — the unity and harmony of forms, unity in variety, significance of forms, their expressiveness. And one still cannot be certain that these terms would be univocal in the context of each of the media. All these considerations show that the idea of art is indefinable.

Instead of accepting this conclusion, one can follow another avenue of discussion that is open. This is a more roundabout way. And it is initially subjective. We begin by ascertaining what manner of approach we take to any of the arts. Could this manner of relating ourselves to works of art give us a clue to the nature of the object on which we focus our interest and thereby allow us to arrive at a view of the value that works of art have for us? (While the method is initially attitudinal and thus perhaps subjective, the question returns us to an examination of the object again and may give us an approach to a definition of the value of art.)

II

We begin with a dogma in the philosophy of art: that works of art are objects that have intrinsic worth. We usually take this to mean that we are not to consider them as objects of only ulterior (or extrinsic) value. This is not to say that a building or a song will not have extrinsic values and ulterior uses. But *qua* art, they must have an intrinsic worth. This is the sort of status a teabowl has for a Zen master. He drinks tea out of it, and the ritual and the utensil have religious significance, but the teabowl is also appreciated as an object of beauty on its own. Thus, there is a moment in the tea ceremony when the host and the guest fondle, appreciate and savor the shape, texture, color and personality of the teabowl, ritualistically. In taking an object as having intrinsic value, our attitude towards that object must be disinterested and contemplative. (Aesthetic theories that have tried to define the aesthetic attitude have all come to some conclusion as this, and thus this statement too, has the status of a dogma.)[2] This stipulation must not deceive us. Taking a distanced attitude does not mean that we cannot be carried away by the strong, infective impact of a piece of music or a play. It simply means that in a response that is appropriate to a work of art, we must not be oblivious to or confused about our identity or the nature, quality and tone of our passional experiences; that is, we must hold on to our critical faculties. If, for example, at the performance of a play, we are made so ill by the violence on the stage that we vomit or lose consciousness, the play has affected us; but it has not been effective *as* a work of art. If, like Don Quixote, we forget ourselves and rush on the stage to save the damsel in distress, the play seems not to differ from a psycho-drama. To take a disinterested view does not mean, of course, that we must be indifferent. There *must,* naturally, be an interest. Only it is the sort that we call "disinterested" or "dis-passionate." The reverse of this theoretical coin is that if we cannot "take" (i.e. view) these objects or events for what they are, they fail as works of art. In saying that a response is defective and incomplete, we mean that the work of art is not functioning as art (autonomous and yielding an independent value of its own). We are responding to it on our own terms, as we wish to see it. Such subjective responses vary among persons as well as periods. We frequently describe this difference by the misleading label of "differences in acquired tastes." But responses vary greatly; and they may be wildly irrelevant or unusual and idiosyncratic responses, which are nevertheless plausible, or they may be simply partial and inadequate. The novels of James Fenimore Cooper, for example, can be read as thrilling tales about Indians or, as D. H. Lawrence read them, as a "yearning myth"

131

embodying our attitude toward the meaning of life in the New World.[3] A person may see only propaganda art and sexualism in *Tristam und Isolde* or, as Nietzsche did, he may view it as the height of Apollonian art. (At this stage, I am only indicating the difference in responses; I wish to suggest nothing about the adequacy of any of them.) One or both may be right in either case. It depends on whether on repeated experience, the responses continue to fit the work of art. Some objects, perhaps, like sections of Joyce's *Finnegans Wake*,[4] may raise such high barriers and may be so ambiguous that they not only give rise to many different responses but may also be unrewarding, ultimately, to continued study.

However, we must respond to works of art, and in a certain manner; and I see no objections to describing this process as "contemplating a work of art," though perhaps in some cases, the response is too highly charged emotionally (like our response to the climax of *Oedipus Rex*) for this relatively cool term. The movement in our response may be too wide and active to be called "contemplation," as when we scan a ceiling by Tiepolo, and it seems even odder to say that we contemplate a poem or a novel. Although in all cases we must respond with our critical eyes active, the responses differ enormously. Bellini's *I Puritani* and Verdi's *Otello* embody different degrees of emotionality; no one can be cool at the climax of *Otello,* act III, in the sequence where Othello insults and curses Desdemona, as he might be in the mad scene of *I Puritani* (act III). Both are musical works and both are operas; and although both are emotional, *Otello* has added violence and embodiment of energy missing in *I Puritani.* An active respondent will be aware of this difference. This awareness, however, must be tempered (both on the part of the spectator as well as the creator or performer) by critical acumen and an inner watchfulness, as much in the bel canto singing of *I Puritani* as in *Otello.* It is this controlled scrutiny that one might wish to indicate by the use of the term contemplation. [5]

What is it that we contemplate? Many different features; the sensuous qualities, the structures, the propulsive movement that these works of art present. Also we must consider that elusive thing which we call musical significance. For this, because of the variety, we need different skills. In music we encounter both natural and artificial sounds (though more of the latter) to which we attend as sheer sounds, as pitches, harmonics and timbre, and as organizations small and large. Our task is to grasp what is there and to perceive what the sounds are. Works of art strike us variously, for they differ with the style and vision of each artist. Sometimes what we see seems to be presented to us matter-of-factly (early Monet, Pissarro) or in an idealized and purified way (Poussin and Claude Lorraine), or personally, painfully, brutally (Grünewald, George Grosz). Our task is to savor these differences accurately. (If we do not want to do so, we might as well leave the works of art alone.) Sometimes, what we notice predominantly, as in the case of the works of the expressionists (Kokoschka, Nolde) is our emotional reaction. This reaction is even more heightened by the works of the action painters. In perusing them, our perceptual and emotional reactions come to us fused, and this fusion seems to be the important thing to attend to. In such cases, we appear to be looking at ourselves.

Works of art are artifacts. Their first requirement is that they be arresting. They must be of interest — spellbinders. But we must get something out of the entrancement they bring. In order to make the most of it, one has to be sensitive to the minutest nuances, even the bad ones; moreover, one needs to be capable of accounting for and estimating his own emotional responses accurately. An ideal critic is one who can help a less practiced person attain this entrancement by describing, analyzing, interpreting a work of art; and this is a rehearsal, in detail, of the process that he goes through in responding to a work on any other level. He talks, of course, but we gain much by his *presence*. He needs to point, to dramatize, in order to activate the imagination of the listener — for looking at a work of art requires undivided contemplation and a generous heart. The viewer need not bring anything but himself[6] — the work of art being the all-important thing — but the viewer must *open* himself.

It is possible, if we wish, to say that an acute observer (or the critic) exercises his imagination in seeing a piece of the world as presented in the work of art — some works apparently simple, like Mondrian, a little Mozart sonata or a Japanese ritual dance; some more complex, like the *Guernica*, the *Brothers Karamazov* or Alban Berg's *Wozzeck*. We sit and watch, listen to or contemplate these objects, taking them for what they are. In this process, we see new orderings, new presentations, strange seas of thought, unfathomed depths of emotionality. Art then, is an instrument by which we see and live imaginatively and share the expressions and visions of others. This sharing obviously involves the artist. But it also brings in other viewers, in proportion as the community is composed of acute, sensitive, disciplined and adequate connoisseurs. To the extent that the formal and harmonious structuring (and sometimes the sensuous coverings) of a work of art causes us to react to it appropriately, i.e. keep us spellbound, the work of art is a satisfactory one. Works of art, then, must not only catch us but they must also hold us.

The play of imagination in this context is worth exploring in detail. In our hurried, animal existence, we perceive (probably) all that we need to perceive in our experiences. Usually, however, we do not "see" aesthetically. Rather, we devour our experiences greedily and anxiously as symptoms of something else—red for blood, for danger, for a persimmon; a large dark oval for an automobile, a building in the distance, all of them of interest to the extent that they connect with the future fulfillment of a present desire. But we may respond in another way. We do so when we pause to notice that a group of buildings, a park or a sunset is beautiful. The usefulness of so doing may be doubtful. But initially we may say that we enjoy doing so. It is pleasant to be thrilled by a sunset, the play of sunlight on the dark leaves in a park. So also with paintings and music. But a better (because more significant) answer is possible.[7] It could be developed out of two further dogmas in aesthetics: first that works of art communicate (though no telling what); second, that works of art humanize us.[8] If either of these two functions takes place, it comes about through the imagination. In order for our perception of a work of art to be adequate, it must be a complete, full seeing. Thereby we suspend the hurried, schematic reading which is our quotidian seeing of things and events. Our aesthetic responses permit us to evaluate, to take stock of the actual immediate qualities of our experiences and our lives. Art humanizes us because it compels us to scrutinize our responses to the world in its thick, independent fullness. In most cases it is not the *ordinary* world, as such, because what we see in a work of art has been selected, fused and transmuted by the imagination of the artist. It is an artist's vision. It may or may not be ordinary. But our attitude to it is certainly not ordinary, for to our world we have a habitual way of responding; our response to that world is mechanical and teleological, geared to the limited bounds of our special preoccupations, obsessions and tastes. The aesthetic situation itself evokes in us this special attitude in the presence of a work of art. In making us take it on its own terms, it breaks the arc of utility, and we emerge from *ourselves* for the moment, assuming a "dis-interested," non-egocentric stance. The reverse side of this coin is the notion of empathy. In it too, we are humanized because, for once, we discard our narrow identity; we fuse our own self and the vision we experience. This process may go under the name of communication, for thereby we gain something. To be arrested in such a stance, even for a brief moment, has a therapeutic value.

As described so far, the aesthetic commerce perhaps sounds a bit too tranquil. But the work of art present can vary the quality of this vision and attitude. A work of art can provoke the agony, the entanglement, the depth of feeling that life demands and creates, as well as the humor in the ironic turns of events or the tragedy in the bitter reversals of causes. Works of art, better than any work of discursive reason, can enmesh a person in the deep confrontation with a vision of the possibilities that life holds. Such presentations have a way of turning into moral visions. To present, for example, a vivid, concrete picture of the agony of being a man in a world of automation can have subtle, important, though perhaps not immediate, results. An aesthetic response is not necessarily a tranquilizer; far from it.

But this description still excludes the entanglement, the loss of self that we experience in a gripping novel or a film. Sometimes we *want* to be swept along, and Wagnerian operas, jazz, the climax of certain dramas do this. To say that works of art communicate is not enough. Rather, we must say that they transform us. Important works of art have packed in them such a thrust that they metamorphose our experience and consciousness. They provoke a gut response sometimes, and in such an aesthetic transaction, we give all of ourselves, we hold back nothing. But how accurate is the aesthetics of total emotional involvement? Such involvement is not, first of all, unique to aesthetic experience. We can find involvement and commitment in political and moral activity as well, in which case we must act, but the better part of wisdom is to retain our critical faculties intact. The idea of total involvement in a work of art intends a dissolution of the distinction that one might draw between the world of art and the ordinary world. We must be wholly immersed in our experience because we want art to *mean* something to us, and the usual aesthetic attitude is not vital enough. But such an involvement — even if it is simply that of placing the paint on the canvas — and the identity and immersion of ordinary experience and aesthetic experience, introduce the notion of practicality and action into the aesthetic process. In support of such a view, one can say that frequently

135

overt action has resulted from our experience of works of art. (Beaumarchais's *Marriage of Figaro* is said to be related to the causes of the French Revolution.) But aesthetically more significant, the practical consequences may include changes in the forms of our future perceptions and reactions, not only to works of art but to other things. Our reactions to picketers in a strike differ crucially from our reactions to a play about picketers in a strike. In the latter we evaluate our experiences critically *for what they are.*[9] (Though the author may spell out a chain of causes, we are asked to see clearly what they amount to. There are no practical differences that should matter to us.) We savor what is presented to us and also the manner of presentation. A loss of self, however, prevents the possibility of our doing it accurately. In the rush of events, say, when we take part in a riot, when we are swept along, we lose the very critical acumen, that capacity to observe exactly what is going on, that an aesthetic scrutiny requires. Psychologically there seems to be a gap between involvement and observation — enough to have led people to say that works of art are nonpractical. And there is as much truth to that statement as there is in any aesthetic dogma.

Works of art, then, present the feel of life and nature for direct contemplation, and the stuff of life is relayed to us by an artist through his imagination. But so stated, the conclusion is inadequate and ultimately misleading. It suggests that the relation of art to human experience is some form of correspondence. The artist takes some portion of our experience of life, and in another medium, he presents a semblance of it. We reinterpret and read it as a form of imitation which leads back to the original experience it resembles. And our common presupposition about art is in accordance with this. We frequently stand bewildered before a work of art and ask what is it, but we would be irritated if we were given an answer such as "just what it is." There are works of art in which we do not, at first glance, recognize anything; yet upon scrutiny, if we suddenly recognize something, we are delighted. Such is the experience of suddenly seeing the surface embossment of a bronze urn of the Shang dynasty to be the stylized mask of a dragon (though it may also continue to look like an abstract filigree). If we were to ask, with reference to a Persian mosaic what it is, the reply would be: an arabesque. A design? We knew that all along. But this is the right answer because what we have before us is a decorative pattern — something entirely independent of anything else.[10] It is not trying to

136

suggest anything, so the right answer is a rejection of the question. But later, when we are looking at other things, nature might begin to suggest, to reverse the process, the Persian arabesque. Sometimes nature imitates art.[11]

The tradition in the practice of the art and crafts does not support the thesis that all art is imitation. It is frequently said that the ultimate symbol of Egyptian civilization, the tomb, *suggests* the psychological space of death; and that the symbol of Gothic culture, the cathedral, suggests the upward rising spaces of heaven (and man's aspiration towards it).[12] But a more accurate view is that these entities actually create what they suggest: i.e., form it for the first time. It *is* what it is, it does not merely suggest it. A Grecian urn does not suggest calmness and harmony. It is calmness and harmony because it creates them, and both calmness and harmony come into being while we look at the urn. In many works of art, the material manifestation is what is most significant, and the matter out of which a work is created is not mimetic. In all works of art the substance, the form and the meaning are inseparable. Thus, if we were to emphasize the material originality and concreteness of works of art,[13] the mimetic theory is inadequate. In our cognition of a work of art, the substance as a medium can begin to articulate the whole meaning of the work of art. What is Bernini's statue of Constantine? A lump of bronze. Bronze arranged to form a solid volume to fill up space. Further the structure brings into play and commands a great part of the space around it. The sculpture is thus not only the matter which it is made out of (which is concrete and particular) but also the space it breathes in and which it requires to appear to full advantage. It breathes; the space around it moves, and this, too, is a part of the statuary. Though the space, as empty space, would be there even if the statue were not there, its life and breath come into being with the presence of the statue. This example of baroque statuary is unique in having as a part of it a backdrop of bronze drapery. The effect comes from its being a gesture of bravura — bronze flesh and bronze tapestry— not from its being a copy of anything or the creation of an illusion. It is bronze, we see. It is shaped. It creates a space — a moving space — and a volume and a heroic gesture. Although it happens to represent a man on a horse and both men and horse bear names, one can go a long way and get the essential meaning of this statuary without knowing the identity of the objects. It would, of course, be silly to ignore these facts, since knowing them speeds the process of comprehending this work, but still what is essential in comprehending this object is to see what it is concretely, materially, sensuously and emotionally. This manner of viewing a sculpture of Bernini can be transferred to a non-objective sculture, for example, a figure by Roszak or a stabile by Calder; or to architectural facades and architectural unit designs — like Borromini's *San Carlino alle Quattro Fontane* or Bernini's St. Peter's colonade — or to something nonmaterial like a play, where each occasion becomes a related but original creation. For example, each performance of *Hamlet* is a different occasion, embodying interesting and important differences that are essentialy significant, especially if the actors and production are different.

Whether a work benefits from a permanent embodiment or not, for the fundamental understanding of a work of art, we must return (and if possible keep returning) to the original object or reenactment, and not to some external reference or resemblance. This is true even in the literary arts. Frequently, a novel is praised for depicting accurately the way things are as if that were its chief function (or even among its significant functions). Such comments presuppose that the art of the novel is a transcription of a prior experience. But in actuality, if that is all that a novel does, we should not need to go to it at all, except as a source for biographical information. Although we often praise a novel for depicting vividly how a person is and acts, that is a distortion of what the critic wishes to say. The novel creates (and shows us) a man of a certain sort and shows him in action. In reading, we recognize people like him in life. A literary work of art creates, and it is a revelation for the reader in exactly the same way that a nonliterary work of art is for one who views or hears it. That the events and characters in a novel are "real" is no reason for praising it; nor is the fact that the events and characters are "unreal" any reason for rejecting a novel. Often the characters of a novel are real because they seem to have an existence of their own. The verisimilitude of the characters, situations and setting in a novel contributes to the cohesion and unity of the work. Good novels are good in a multitude of ways. Poor novels are poor because they are incomplete and shallow—they are not worthy of scrutiny.

Some generalizations:

A) A work of art is a member of a class of objects (or events) that has survived (perhaps countless) acts of scrutiny and contemplation and shown itself to yield fully satisfactory results on being treated aesthetically.

B) To treat an object aesthetically is to treat it as an object in itself, as an object (or sequence of qualities and events) of intrinsic interest.   (The notion of the aesthetic is framed from the side of the spectator, not that of the creator.)

C) An experience that is satisfactory must fulfill two conditions: (1) The first is a formal condition: an experience must fulfill itself — that is round itself off (more or less) satisfactorily. It must show itself to be organized, harmonious; it must bring one's communion with a work of art to a definite close.   (2) The experience must be significant so that the act of attention seems worthwhile. The experience may have the character of a refreshment; an occasion that is sensuously bracing, rich and rewarding (works that give us this kind of experience we typically call delightful, charming, decorative, etc.); but we treasure more those works that embody meanings that reveal to us a depth and height of human experience previously unsuspected by us. To the extent that works of art are satisfactory, in the second way, we forgive formal imperfections in style, medium, in structure, etc.

D) A corollary: The results that we expect from our interaction with works of art are varied. But on the primary sensuous level it is to acquire an immediate awareness of an imaginative configuration which is also an independent world; one that is not merely a copy of our own but an original vision. And this vision on a higher level should broaden and enrich our acquaintance with our world by becoming a part of it. Such transactions would result in a fuller realization of our humanity, in rebirth. The process of adequately responding to a work of art is difficult and requires patient study and training. But short of a religious experience, nothing else would give us such results.

III

There is a commerce, an imaginative interchange, between works of art and human beings. It is worthwhile to tally up the fruits and profits of this commerce. What do human beings gain from this transaction? What I wish to argue is that the effect of works of art on us is moral, though *moral* in a relatively broad sense.

139

They sometimes please us, sometimes refresh us. If this were all, then the results seem dispensable. But delight and enchantment seem not to be true of *all* works of art. Nor do all works of art lead to a cathartic flushing out of the anxieties that spring from the suppression of prohibited desires. Neither do they all unite us in a bond of universal brotherhood; nor do they all hold up a mirror to nature, showing us how man may be merged into nature.

In the generalizations given above, the strongest effect of art on the human spirit was claimed to consist in the demand of objectivity that it imposes. By this I mean that in the communion with a work of art, what is required of the observer is a clarity of response (no matter how ambiguous and confused the *work itself* may be). And it is obvious that no clarity, as such, is possible if the agent is not aware of his own responses and does not bring them under his own cognition; nor can there be any clarity if he is not capable of accuracy, precision and control *in the seeing* itself. The sum of this discipline we call "taking the work of art for what it is." When we consider the matter, we realize that very few objects and events in the world demand this discipline of men and allow this objectivity to come into play successfully. The interpretation of public events, the reaffirmation of the mores of a community, the moral evaluation of our motives, the writing of history, the construction of a scientific theory — all of these lead us in different directions, for they involve the pursuit of various goals or the achievement of an abstract form. (Though geared to accuracy and truth, science moves away from the concrete, particularity of events.)

The predominent quotidian patterns of our lives are pragmatic, consummatory and utilitarian. But there is also non-consummatory behavior — being a philosopher, a gymnast or a saint. They all require patient, slow, single-minded cultivation. The capacity to respond adequately to works of art is also a mode that calls for development. Although the clarity and truthfulness of seeing involved fall within the range of rationality, it is not discursive, because words and concepts are not adequate to it. To see our experiences wholly and steadily *is* a work of reason, although this region of reason is not cut off from feeling. Some thoughts after all are inseparable from the feelings that accompany them; some emotional responses are appropriate to them and others are not. As we have seen, the complexity of many works of art fully controls the range of feelings that may arise on a full confrontation with *the* work of art. That is how works of art are constructed.

Notice that the idea of an aesthetic attitude, i.e., that of treating an object or event as having intrinsic value, when elaborated fully, moves toward the notion of autonomy. But instead of proceeding with the idea of aesthetic autonomy and reiterating concepts that have been gone over already, it would help, at this point, to extend the discussion beyond the realm of art. A helpful corollary to art as autonomous is the idea of a human being as autonomous. That a person is autonomous (an entity with intrinsic dignity) is the answer that we glibly give to the question; namely, what is the proper way to treat a person? (The parallel has been suggested earlier in connection with the notion of uniqueness, Chapter 6.) What is the proper way to treat a human being? We often answer, rather airily: treat him as a person. The possibilities are still very wide. For example, in treating a person as a person, must we like him? Must we love him, as commanded in holy scripture? He might be unlovable. In treating a being as a person, we should (to use a Kantian locution) treat him, before all else, as an end in himself, and as a responsible, free agent. This task, not an easy one, is usually helped by one's ability to see the person fully as he is. There is no simple way to do this, for we must avoid approaching him with a preconceived idea, a stereotype, a label, a role, all ready in our mind; but rather to try to understand him as he truly is, complex and perhaps inscrutable. It helps in this context to assume that he is unique and to let this assumption rule our relation with him. It must be admitted that the occasions when we must do this is infrequent. It would be both tiresome as well as time consuming to relate to anyone and everyone as autonomous persons. Employers see their employees in terms of the work they are expected to do; teachers, their pupils in terms of their studies; and we (as consumers) must see the various waiters, clerks, cashiers, etc., in terms of the roles they must perform as we meet them in our daily lives.

But in the autonomy context, to care about a person is to understand him. And to understand a person, we must, apart from our own predispositions, let him be himself, his own being. The chief example that would come to our mind here from our own common experience is that of our friends, those to whom we have been very close and whom we have known a long time, and those whose actions, no matter what they do, cease to sur-

141

prise us (not because they are predictable, but because we simply accept them). Only rarely do members of our own family count here, because our relationship to them is pre-established by blood and family ties — i.e., roles. Most of us know very little about our parents or our siblings. To know anyone closely and fully takes time. But this is also to love him. In any such relation, our interest, our care, our desires come into play, naturally; but where love is concerned, we must lose ourselves. Our loss of self comes about because we have let the being of the object realize itself — to come into being and to engulf us.[14] The relationship is purely intrinsic, and contingent on the being (nature) of the two persons involved. Sexual desire and romantic love are both irrelevant in this context, for the former is goal-oriented and consummatory; and romantic love is controlled by an abstract notion. Love between two autonomous beings is a relationship which grows in an atmosphere of mutual regard, respect and freedom. In this sense, love is objective and an activity open only to rational beings.

Love is often identified with desire, as in Plato's *Symposium*,[15] where it is said that love is a type of desire for an object which we lack but which is thought to be good. But desire *per se* as a paradigm of love does not apply to a person who loves mathematics, his country (although one may say that what one desires is the glory and greatness of his country, or the continuation of this glory and greatness), a work of art that one is comtemplating, or a loved one where the love is requited. "For many things are born out of a person's love: desire, thought, volition, action. All these things, however, which grow from love, like the harvest from a seed, are not love itself, but rather presuppose its existence."[16] Love, like a desire, begins in restlessness (that grows out of a lack) but while desire is satisfied by a taking-in — a mouth-oriented ingestion — love is other-directed. There are many things we desire which we do not love, and most things that we desire, we no longer desire after obtaining them. But we expect love to endure the achievement of the object. When we love a work of art, a person, or even some item of food — olives, for example — we expect the outward reaching, the yearning, the interest to be constant, because we expect it to be conditioned by a full and adequate cognition of the object of love. Love and liking (which resemble each other and are often confused) differ in this respect: liking can alight on anything, but love is contingent on the properties of the object. We can,

142

of course, say I like John Smith because he has cute pointed ears that wiggle whenever he is irritated. Of course, we can say and explain what it is that *makes us* like a person and do so by giving causal reasons. But there are no reasons as such.[17] Love, on the other hand, is not merely affective; it is grounded on thought and reflection.

In final analysis, it is not easy to love. We encounter our objects of love — our parents, our brothers and sisters, our homes, our cities, our country, our God — in the tyrannous context of a culture and a society; and in such contexts, passion or the mechanism of habit are encouraged, not love. We are taught to love truthfully (what we colloquially though misleadingly call "true love") first of all, as a matter of fact, by works of art and the experience of the beautiful in general. This capacity is best, because most easily, developed, if we allow it, in the aesthetic context. Having learned it there, we may extend it to other cases including human beings. The reverse is so very difficult that it is really impossible. For example, we are naturally required by social conditions to treat persons in special ways: as a shopkeeper, as a policeman, as a child, as a mother or as a superior, and we readily think of these relationships as grounded in morality. And it is too easy to think of morality as religiously sanctioned or as a tool of society. It is not easy to break out of these routines. But our care and communion with works of art can teach us to treat human beings with care and love.

Works of art as well as human beings are unique and have intrinsic value. Therefore, we must respond to both imaginatively, with full insight and open hearts. In exercising our aesthetic attitude towards works of art, we learn to treat things as ends in themselves and we practice living a full life of the imagination. In our human relationships, too, we attempt to work our heart and imagination to the fullest. Despite the aesthetic parallel, this is not to treat human beings "aesthetically" in a pejorative sense. There are two ways in which persons can be treated aesthetically. It would be undesirable to transform persons into objects of "taste." That would not be to treat people as persons, but as an "object," a thing; to see them as means to something else — usually occasions to discharge certain feelings or emotions, on our part. Our interest is focussed on our feeling, in such cases, not on the person. But there is another (correct) sense of "aesthetic" in which to treat a person "aesthetically" means to see him as a whole and as a source of intrinsic worth, *proper to itself,* and the sort of entity he is. This treatment involves seeing his various qualities accurately, estimating their connections truly; letting his character as a whole have full impact on us; allowing his full being to come into play before we make an estimation, and when we make an estimation, to do so in the light of all that we relevantly know of him; and ultimately granting his right to his own form of authenticity. Of course there are incomplete persons: persons who are fractured, persons who are corrupt, persons who are so rigid and habit-ridden that in our interactions with them we find little that is interesting or lovable. Like disorganized works of art, or works of art that are defective, they show their faults. They turn out to be non-autonomous. Our experiences with them tend to be incomplete, unhappy, destructive; and the experiences refuse to round themselves off. But the clarity and accuracy of perception (thus our capacity to love) must come first. Ultimately, I believe that this is the only morality that there can be; and any moral relation is one that must be grounded on such a generous heart.

On the view that I have developed, the steadiness, endurance and strength in our capacity to respond is developed by art. It has a function that is related to that of religion and (in a broad sense) moral philosophy; and it is a task that systems of logical thought or science are not intended to perform. Indeed, they cannot perform it. The fact that we live in a society necessarily and inevitably raises many limits and controls over our actions. We have to get along, earn our bread and rear our families. It is difficult to reconcile these duties with the sheer freedom that we sometimes (perhaps mistakenly) feel to be our right. Sometimes we even feel that our very rationality must consist in the realization of this freedom. Works of art frequently assuage and satisfy our drive and thirst for autonomy, for great works of art are such autonomous, free creatures, containing within themselves their own necessary being. Unfortunately, there are few works of art, they are hard to create, and when they come into being, they do so with difficulty as if they did not wish to come into existence. But that is because, after all, there is a strain in the idea of a work of art. There must be, if the ideas of form and autonomy, controlled creation and freedom, sensuous immediacy and significance, are all contained within a single entity.

144

NOTES

CHAPTER I

1. Plato, *Meno,* St. 80A.

CHAPTER 2

1. Water Pater, *The Renaissance, Studies in Art and Poetry* (London, 1893), p. 61.
2. *Ibid.,* p. 112.
3. *Ibid.,* p. 124.
4. *Ibid.,* pp. 131—132.
5. R. P. Blackmur, *Language as Gesture* (New York, 1952), p. 382.
6. See Herbert Read, *The Philosophy of Modern Art* (New York, 1953), pp. 17ff. (In connection with Pater on Mona Lisa, Freud's comments on it in *Leonardo da Vinci: A study in Psychosexuality* should be interesting.)
7. D. H. Lawrence, *Studies in Classical American Literature* (New York, 1951), p. 93.
8. *Ibid.,* p. 12.
9. *Ibid.,* pp. 12—13.
10. *Ibid.,* p. 17.
11. F. R. Leavis, *D. H. Lawrence* (Cambridge, 1930), p. 12.
12. Lawrence, *Studies,* p. 146.
13. *Ibid.,* p. 148.
14. Herbert Read, p. 66.
15. Archibald MacLeish, "Ars Poetica," in *Collected Poems* (Boston, 1952), p. 41.

16. The Detroit Art Institute, *Flanders in the 15th Century: Art and Civilization / Catalogue of the Exhibition / Masterpieces of Flemish Art: Van Dyck to Bosch* (Detroit, 1960), p. 69.
17. Giorgio Vasari, *Lives of the Painters Sculptors and Architects,* 4 vols. (London, 1927), IV, 162.
18. William Empson, *Seven types of Ambiguity,* rev. ed. (London, 1949), p. 211.
19. See the various essays in Irwin Panofsky, *Studies in Iconology* (New York, 1939) and in *Meaning in the Visual Arts* (New York, 1955).
20. Empson, pp. 212—213.
21. *Ibid.,* p. 235.
22. *Ibid.,* pp., 245—246.
23. See, for example, D. F. Tovey, *A Companion to Beethoven's Pianoforte Sonatas* (Complete Analyses) (London, 1935).

CHAPTER 3

1. I am using the word "enjoying" in a sense in which it is *not* equivalent to mere liking or the simple taking of pleasure in something. In Chapter 7, I use this term in a cruder sense.
2. Virgil Thomson, "Music in Review" in *The New York Herald Tribune,* March 20, 1949.
3. John Ruskin, *Modern Painters* in *Works* (London, 1903), III, 571.
4. Edwin Denby, "Three sides of Agon" in the program of the *Tenth Anniversary of the New York City Ballet* (New York [1958]), [p. 4].
5. Roger Fry, *Vision and Design* (New York, 1947), pp. 125, 136.
6. *Ibid.,* p. 109.
7. *Ibid.,* p. 151.
8. W. J. Turner, *Mozart* (New York, 1938), p. 384.
9. Rosemary Hughes, *Haydn* (London, 1950), p. 165.
10. Fry, *Vision and Design,* p. 102.
11. D. F. Tovey, *Essays in Musical Analysis: Chamber Music* (London, 1944), p. 94.
12. *Ibid.,* p. 38.
13. Frank Sibley, "Aesthetic Concepts" in *Philosophical Review,* LXVIII, 421—450.
14. Sometimes we want to say that non-aesthetic properties are objective; but the aesthetic ones are subjective (and perhaps dependent on the perceiver's emotional responses.) This way of differentiating them gives short shrift to the various ways in which questions about aesthetic properties may be adjudicated.
15. Tovey, p. 102.
16. Program notes, *Tenth Anniversary of the New York City Ballet,* p. 38.
17. Fry, *Vision and Design,* p. 125.
18. B. H. Haggin, *The Listener's Musical Companion* (New Brunswick, N.J., 1956), p. 98.

19. Denby, Program, *Tenth Anniversary of the New York City Ballet,* pp. 4—5.
20. Albert Schweitzer, *J. S. Bach* (London, 1947), II, 105.
21. Edmund Wilson, *The Wound and the Bow* (New York, 1959), p. 75.
22. S. E. Toulmin and K. Baier, "On Describing" in *Mind,* n.s., LXI, 14, 19—20.
23. Ruskin, pp. 571—572.
24. Herbert Read, *Philosophy of Modern Art,* p. 82.
25. Petronius Arbiter in Helen Waddell, *Medieval Latin Lyrics* (London, 1948), p. 19.
26. Sigmund Freud, *The Interpretation of Dreams* in *The Basic Writings of Sigmund Freud,* tr. and ed. by A.A. Brill (New York, 1938), pp. 207, 188, 192, 205.
27. I use the word "utterance" to include not only *what* is said but where, when, how, etc., it is said.
28. Margaret Macdonald in the Symposium: "What are the distinctive features of arguments in Art Criticism?" in the *Aristotetian Society,* supplementary volume, XXIII, pp. 192—193, with Miss Macdonald, A. N. Hannay and John Holloway as participants. Miss Macdonald's contribution is reprinted with important additions in William Elton, *Aesthetics and Language* (Oxford, 1954), pp. 114—130.
29. Roland Penrose in the exhibition catalogue of the Arts Council of Great Britain, 1960, *Picasso* (London, 1960), p. 49.
30. Marya Mannes, "Just Looking, Thanks" in *The Reporter,* October 13, 1960, p. 48.
31. From the program notes for a concert by the Concertgebouw Orchestra of Amsterdam, The University of Michigan Musical Society, complete series 3141.
32. Macdonald *et al,* p. 167.
33. G. M. Hopkins, *Poems,* 3rd ed. (Oxford, 1948), p. 109.
34. *Ibid.,* p. 73.
35. Macdonald *et al.,* p. 171.
36. Macdonald in Elton *Aesthetics,* p. 126.
37. Elton, *Aesthetics,* pp. 126-127.
38. *Ibid.,* pp. 127-128.
39. *Ibid.,* p. 130.
40. *Ibid.,* p. 129.
41. Fry, *Vision and Design,* p. 107.

CHAPTER 4

1. Wallace Stevens, *Harmonium* (New York, 1950), p. 153.
2. Gustave Flaubert, *Madame Bovary,* tr. by Francis Steegmuller (New York, 1957), p. 251.
3. *Ibid.,* pp. 253-254.
4. Leo Tolstóy, *What is Art? and Essays on Art* (Oxford, 1930), p. 228.
5. D. W. Prall, *Aesthetic Analysis* (New York, 1936), pp. 78—82.

6. Gilbert Ryle, "Feelings" in Elton, *Aesthetics and Language,* pp. 56-72. See also Gilbert Ryle, "Pleasure" in his *Dilemmas* (Cambridge, 1960), pp. 54—67.
7. Peter Latham, *Brahms* (London, 1949), p. v.
8. Jack Kroll in his exhibition reviews in *The Art News,* LX, no. 3, p. 13.
9. *Ibid.* pp. 10-11.
10. Bernard Heyl, "The Critics' Reasons," *Journal of Aesthetics and Art Criticism,* XVI, 174.
11. See George Santayana, *Sense of Beauty* (New York, 1896), pp. 35—41; and Kant in the *Critique of Judgment,* Second Moment, § 8.
12. The coining of the term "aesthetic" is usually attributed to Baumgarten, ca. 1750, and by it he meant the science of sensible knowledge.

CHAPTER 5

1. D. F. Tovey, *Essays in Musical Analysis* (Oxford, 1948) III, 3.
2. Virginia Woolf, *The Common Reader* (New York, 1948), pp. 126—127.
3. F. R. Leavis, *The Great Tradition* (London, 1948), p. 1.
4. Roger Fry, *French, Flemish and British Art* (New York, 1951), pp. 137—138.
5. Gisela Richter, *Ancient Italy* (Ann Arbor, 1955), p. 12. Even this quotation seems to suggest that the statuary under consideration is an *artistic* monument of some importance. In 1961, it was announced by the Metropolitan Museum that this item plus two others were fakes.
6. A. J. Ayer, *Language, Truth and Logic* (London, 1948), p. 113.
7. B. H. Haggin, *The Listener's Musical Companion* (New Brunswick, N.J., 1956), p. 64.
8. The word "preference" is ambiguous. It has a comparative and a non-comparative use.
9. John Pope-Hennessy, *Giovanni di Paolo* (New York, 1939), pp. 148—149.
10. Leavis, p. 19.
11. Fry, *Art,* pp. 123—128.
12. *Ibid.,* p. 124.
13. *Ibid.,* p. 124.
14. *Ibid.,* p. 126.
15. *Ibid.,* p. 126.
16. *Ibid.,* p. 125.
17. *Ibid.,* p. 127.
18. *Ibid.,* p. 125. These comments in the essay actually refer not to St. Ursula but to the *Adoration of the Magi,* but the point would still be the same.
19. Fry, *Art,* p. 127.
20. *Ibid.,* p. 128.
21. *Ibid.,* pp. 125—126.
22. *Ibid.,* p. 127.
23. *Ibid.,* p. 126.

24. Adolf Rosenberg, *P. P. Rubens* (Berlin [1905]), p. 234.
25. Margaret Macdonald, "Some Distinctive Features of Arguments used in Art Criticism," *Aesthetics and Language,* ed. by William Elton (Oxford, 1954), p. 129. See also Stuart Hampshire, "Logic and Appreciation" in the same collection, p. 166.
26. Tovey, *Essays in Musical Analysis,* III, 16, 64, 70—72.
27. T. S. Eliot, *Selected Essays* (New York, 1950), pp. 123—124.
28. *Ibid.,* p. 124.
29. Size, however, may be a very important factor in some paintings. See Max Friedlander, *On Art and Connoisseurship* (Oxford, 1942) pp. 58—63.
30. See Chapter 6, section ii.
31. See Phyllis McGinley, "What makes a 'Children's Classic'?", *The Griffin* VIII, no. 9, p. 12. Compare with Lionell Trilling, "Mansfield Park," *Partisan Review,* XXI, no. 5, pp. 493—494.

CHAPTER 6

1. Kenneth Clark, *Leonardo da Vinci* (Cambridge, 1952), p. 140.
2. Mosco Carner, *Puccini* (New York, 1959), p. ix.
3. See Frank Sibley, "Aesthetic Concepts," *Philosophical Review,* XLVIII, 421—450.
4. See articles by E. A. Gellner, "Ethics and Logic," and R. M. Hare, "Universalizability" in *Proceedings of the Aristotelian Society,* n.s. LV, 296—298.
5. Hare, *Proceedings,* p. 297
6. M. Rostovstzeff, *Rome, a History of the Ancient World* (Oxford, 19......), II, 137.
7. D. F. Tovey, *Essays in Musical Analysis,* III, 179.
8. Kenneth Clark, *Looking at Pictures* (New York, 1960), p. 85.
9. José Ortega y Gassett, *Dehumanization of Art* (New York, 1956), p. 74.
10. Gilbert Murray, *The Classical Tradition in Poetry* (Cambridge, 1927), p. 51.
11. Harold G. Henderson, *An Introduction to Haiku* (New York, 1958), p. 82.
12. Laurence Lerner, *The Truest Poetry* (London, 1960), pp. 187—192.
13. Tovey, *Essays in Musical Analysis,* III, 16—17.
14. Leo Tolstóy, *What Is Art? and Essays on Art* (Oxford, 1930), p. 248.
15. *Ibid.,* p. 249.
16. Aristotle, *Poetics,* 1453A, Bywater translation.
17. See John Gassner, *Treasury of the Theatre* (New York 1956), p. 1061; Louis Martz, "The Saint as Tragic Hero" in *Tragic Themes in Western Literature,* ed. by Cleanth Brooks (New Haven, 1955), pp. 154—155. To claim that Willy Loman represents all the salesmen of America seems in a way not to fit Aristotle's criteria for the hero, though it might do for a morality tragedy, if there are such. That

Willy Loman has this generalized character, however, has been frequently claimed. (See Eric Bentley, "Back to Broadway," *Theatre Arts*, XXXIII, no. 10, p. 13.)

18. Arthur Miller, "Tragedy and the Common Man," *Theatre Arts*, XXXV, no. 3, p. 48.
19. *Ibid.*, p. 48.
20. In some of the arts, for example in painting, the concept of genre seems less well defined. We sometimes call still lifes, landscapes, nudes, Dutch interiors by the name of genre, but are these correctly designated?
21. Michael Ayrton, *"The Music Party*: Watteau" in *Enjoying Paintings*, ed. by David Piper (Harmondsworth, Middlesex, 1964), p. 45.
22. Joseph Conrad, *Chance* (London, 1925), pp. 233—234.
23. C. S. Lewis, *English Literature of the Sixteenth Century* (Oxford, 1954), p. 538.
24. *Ibid.*, p. 539.
25. *Ibid.*, p. 502.
26. See P. H. Nowell-Smith, "Are Historical Events Unique?" *Proceedings of the Aristotelian Society*, n.s., LVII, especially 120—121, and C. B. Joyt and Nicholas Rescher, "The Problem of Uniqueness in History," *History and Theory*, I, no. 2, p. 154.

CHAPTER 7

1. Quoted with names replaced by the letters x and y, from the *Saturday Review*, XLIV, no. 12, p. 54. Oddly enough the comments referred to a phonograph record.
2. Compare what F. R. Leavis says in *The Great Tradition*, p. 2, footnote, with what Ian Watt says, in *The Rise of the Novel* (Berkeley, 1957), pp. 93—94.
3. Berenson's letter in *The Nation*, LXXXVIII, 461 is frequently cited in support of this. Meyer Schapiro argues that Berenson never understood modern art because of his "intellectual and aesthetic narrowness" in an article on "Mr. Berenson's Values" in *Encounter*, XVI, no. 1, pp. 62—63.
4. Francis Henry Taylor, *The Taste of Angels* (Boston, 1948), p. 180.
5. *Ibid.*, pp. 281—290.
6. Dennis Arundell, *The Critic at the Opera* (London, 1957), p. xi.
7. *The Mid-Century* (New York) no. 22 (1961), p. 28.
8. *Ethica Nicomachea*, VII.
9. See Chapter 4, i.
10. Fosco Maraini, *Meeting with Japan* (New York, 1959), pp. 242—244; especially Sir George Sansom, *A History of Japan to 1334* (Stanford, 1958), pp. 178—180, 194.

CHAPTER 8

1. Some versions of the argument have been developed by Morris Weitz, in "The role of theory in Aesthetics," *Journal of Aesthetics and Art Criticism,* XV, 27—35; and Margaret Macdonald, "Art and Imagination," *Proceedings of the Aristotelian Society,* n.s., LIII, 205—226.
2. See, for example, the writings of Edward Bullough and Vernon Lee.
3. D. H. Lawrence, *Studies in Classical American Literature* (New York, 1951), p. 66.
4. See, for example, the long list of despairing critics discussed by J. I. M. Stewart in *Eight Modern Writers* (Oxford, 1963), pp. 479—483.
5. Bellini's melodies have a sustained, well-controlled elegance and simplicity. But as the mad scene progresses, in true cabaletta fashion, the melodies become ornate with complex fioritura. It is then clear that the singer must have a technical control of bravura singing which is a pure activity of the will. But the technical will of the artist needs to be present just as much in the execution of late Verdi-writing, as unornamented as it may seem.
6. A work of art is not normally a projective test.
7. Anyway, hedonism as a philosophy of art is most probably false.
8. B. Berenson, *Aesthetics and History* (New York, 1954), pp. 138—143.
9. We may or may not actually apply standards in such judgments.
10. A pattern, we will suppose here, which is not based on curving vines, tendrils and leaves.
11. Oscar Wilde, *Intentions* (London, 1927), p. 30.
12. Susanne Langer, *Feeling and Form* (New York, 1953), p. 98; and consider especially the use of the term "semblance."
13. By the term "material" I also cover the substance of the drama, the perishing events.
14. Ortega y Gasset says "love envelops the object in a favorable atmosphere"; and that "in love we feel united with the subject." See *On Love* (New York, 1957), p. 18.
15. Plato, *Symposium,* St. 200-201.
16. Ortega y Gasset, p. 11.
17. Because it is not repeatable or universalizable.

TOPICAL INDEX

(Names of artists and works of art mentioned as examples have not been included in the index.)

154

General theory of art, *see* art, general theory

Generalizations
   in art criticism, 83, 98, 111ff.
   in history, 96f., 113f.
   see also universalizability

Genre, 27, 88f., 97, 100, 102
"Good," logical uses of, 76, 118f.
Grading, 25, 96

Hare, R. M., 96
Hegel, 67
Historians as distinguished from scientists, 114
Historical events, uniqueness of, *see* uniqueness of historical events
Historical generalizations, *see* generalizations in history
Historical explanations, 41, 73, 82, 97, 113
   in art criticism, 9f., 21, 82
   see also generalizations in history
Hopkins, G. M., 42, 44
Humanization, art as a means of, 134f.

Identification of a work of art, 27
Imagination, 42, 133, 143
   and imaginative insight, 41f.
Imitation, 136f.
   of a style, 31
Immediacy of sensuous media, *see* medium, immediacy of
Impartiality, 62f., 131, 134f.
Impressionistic criticism, see criticism, impressionistic
Incontinent man, 124
Intentional studies of works of art, 15
Intentionality, 52
Interest, 131
Interpretation, 25, 33, 36f.
   argument-stopping role, 39
   as autobiographical, 41
   corrigibility of, 40f.

as performance, 45
of verbal utterances, 38f.
Intrinsic value, *see* value, intrinsic

Justification
   of attitudes, 68f.
   of feelings, 69
   of responses, 64

Kant, I., 67, 95, 96, 105, 141
Kierkegaard, S., 67

Lawrence, D. H., 15ff., 131
Lewis, C. I., 67
Liking, 25, 74f., 125, 142f.
   logical uses of, 118f.
Logical committment, 75f.
Logical oddness, 118
Love, 141ff.

Marxist analysis, 17, 117
Meaning, 39
   cognitive and noncognitive, 73
Medium, media, 27, 106ff., 130, 137
   immediacy of sensuous media, 107
   of literature, 53, 108f., 138
   as a locus of meaning, 137
   as sensuous materials of art, 53, 106
Miller, Arthur, defense of *Death of a Salesman,* 100f.
Mimesis, *see* imitation
Mood features, 28f., 54
Moral philosophy, 115, 144
Moral reasons, *see* reasons, moral
Moral values, *see* values, moral
Motivational criticism, *see* criticism, contextual
Motivational studies of art, 15
Museums, function of, 121

Names and naming, 27, 33
Nonaesthetic properties, *see* aesthetic concepts
Noncondition-governed criteria, *see* criteria, condition-governed
Noncognitive meaning, *see* meaning, cognitive and noncognitive
Noncritical contexts, *see* critical and noncritical contexts
Nonveridical, *see* corrigibility
Norm, *see* criteria
Novelty, 111

Objective criticism, *see* criticism, rhetorical
Objectivity (and subjectivity)
    of aesthetic judgment, 72ff.
    of attitudes, 68f., 140
    of responses to works of art, 51f., 117

Originality, *see* novelty
Ought and *is,* 83f.

Particularity of a work of art, 107f., 137
Pater, Walter, 11ff., 62
Perceptual activities, 52
Perfection, 111
Performances, 45f., 106
    as creation, 138
    as interpretation, 45
Personal (impersonal and nonpersonal) responses, *see* responses, personal
Personal associations, *see* private associations
Persons, 141
    uniqueness of, 113, 114f.
Physical qualities, 53
Plato, 98
    Meno, 8
    Symposium, 142
Pleasure, 25, 67, 74, 121, 134
    objectified, 51, 67
Pointing gesture, 17, 33, 80, 86

Prall, D. W., on sensuous surfaces, 53
Preference, comparative and noncomparative uses, 74 footnote
Prejudices, 117
Principles, *see* criteria
Privacy of responses, 60
Psychoanalytic interpretations, 37, 43

Read, Herbert, 17, 34
Reasons, 74ff., 118
    aesthetic, 74, 83, 94ff.
    causal, 15, 75, 96, 143
    feature, 78, 83, 111f.
    moral, 96, 143
Reassessment, *see* assessment
Relativity of aesthetic judgments, 73, 90, 118f., 120
Relational theory of value, *see* value
Relevance of reasons, 84, 88
    logical considerations, 90
    psychological considerations, 89
Religion and art, 57, 139, 144
Responses
    corrigibility, 58
    emotional, 51, 54ff.
    personal (impersonal and nonpersonal), 62f.
    subjectivity of, 56
    to a work of art, 10f., 51
Revelation, art as, 138
Rhetorical criticism, *see* criticism, rhetorical
Rules, 101f.
    see also criteria
Ruskin, John, 33f., 62

Sensations, 52f.
Sensitivity, 30
    in taste, 123
    training of, 30, 123